Unsupervised Learning with R

Work with over 40 packages to draw inferences from complex datasets and find hidden patterns in raw unstructured data

Erik Rodríguez Pacheco

PUBLISHING

BIRMINGHAM - MUMBAI

Unsupervised Learning with R

First published: November 2015

Production reference: 1251115

Published by Packt Publishing Ltd.
Livery Place
35 Livery Street
Birmingham B3 2PB, UK.

ISBN 978-1-78588-709-3

www.packtpub.com

Credits

Author
Erik Rodríguez Pacheco

Reviewers
Nicholas A. Yager
Nicolas Turenne

Commissioning Editor
Dipika Gaonkar

Acquisition Editor
Reshma Raman

Content Development Editor
Merwyn D'souza

Technical Editor
Namrata Patil

Copy Editor
Imon Biswas

Project Coordinator
Nikhil Nair

Proofreader
Safis Editing

Indexer
Tejal Soni

Production Coordinator
Manu Joseph

Cover Work
Manu Joseph

About the Author

Erik Rodríguez Pacheco works as a manager in the business intelligence unit at Banco Improsa in San José, Costa Rica, where he holds 11 years of experience in the financial industry. He is currently a professor of the business intelligence specialization program at the Instituto Tecnológico de Costa Rica's continuing education programs. Erik is an enthusiast of new technologies, particularly those related to business intelligence, data mining, and data science. He holds a bachelor's degree in business administration from Universidad de Costa Rica, a specialization in business intelligence from the Instituto Tecnológico de Costa Rica, a specialization in data mining from Promidat (Programa Iberoamericano de Formación en Minería de Datos), and a specialization in business intelligence and data mining from Universidad del Bosque, Colombia. He is currently enrolled in an online specialization program in data science from Johns Hopkins University.

He has served as the technical reviewer of *R Data Visualization Cookbook* and *Data Manipulation with R - Second Edition*, both from Packt Publishing.

He can be reached at https://www.linkedin.com/in/erikrodriguezp.

Acknowledgments

The author of this book is not the creator of any of the packages, functions, or programs used in any of the examples, he is only a facilitator.

For that reason, I would like to sincerely thank the developers of R and R packages, who have contributed so generously to the growing of the R open source community. In this book, we used many packages. Sometimes, the definitions of these packages, in order to be respectful to the authors, are written literally. The Appendix at the end of the book contains all sources as special thanks to the authors.

I would like to thank my data mining professor PhD Oldemar Rodriguez Rojas, who inspired me and taught me so much.

I would also like to thank my publisher, Packt Publishing, for giving me the opportunity to work on this book. I would like to thank all the technical reviewers and content development editors at Packt Publishing for their informative comments and suggestions.

I would like to thank Felix Alpizar Lobo and Irene Gallegos Gurdian from Banco Improsa for all their support and mentoring.

Finally, I would like to thank my amazing wife, Silvia, without her encouragement, support, and patience, this book would not have been possible.

About the Reviewer

Nicholas A. Yager is a biostatistician and software developer researching statistical genomics, image analysis, and infectious disease epidemiology. With an education in biochemistry and biostatistics, his experience analyzing cutting-edge genomics data and simulating complex biological systems has given him an in-depth understanding of scientific computing and data analysis. Currently, Nicholas works for a personalized medicine company, designing medical informatics systems for next-generation personalized cancer tests. Apart from this book, Nicholas has reviewed *Mastering Rstudio: Develop, Communicate, and Collaborate with R, Julian Hillebrand, Maximilian H. Nierhoff, Packt Publishing*.

> I would like to thank my friends, Lauren and Matt, and my mentor, Dr. Gregg Hartvigsen, for their help with this book.

Nicolas Turenne is a PhD in computer science and a research fellow at the French National Institute for Agricultural Research (INRA). He is also in the Interdisciplinary Laboratory Sciences Innovations Societies (LISIS), UMR 1326 at Paris-Est University.

He is an expert in data mining and knowledge discovery from text databases using stochastic and relational models; applications of which are life sciences, security, and social media analysis.

He has written books such as *Knowledge Needs and Information Extraction: Towards an Artificial Consciousness* in March 2013 by Wiley-ISTE and *Analyse de données textuelles sous R*, which will be published in January 2016 by ISTE.

www.PacktPub.com

Support files, eBooks, discount offers, and more

For support files and downloads related to your book, please visit www.PacktPub.com.

Did you know that Packt offers eBook versions of every book published, with PDF and ePub files available? You can upgrade to the eBook version at www.PacktPub.com and as a print book customer, you are entitled to a discount on the eBook copy. Get in touch with us at service@packtpub.com for more details.

At www.PacktPub.com, you can also read a collection of free technical articles, sign up for a range of free newsletters and receive exclusive discounts and offers on Packt books and eBooks.

https://www2.packtpub.com/books/subscription/packtlib

Do you need instant solutions to your IT questions? PacktLib is Packt's online digital book library. Here, you can search, access, and read Packt's entire library of books.

Why subscribe?

- Fully searchable across every book published by Packt
- Copy and paste, print, and bookmark content
- On demand and accessible via a web browser

Free access for Packt account holders

If you have an account with Packt at www.PacktPub.com, you can use this to access PacktLib today and view 9 entirely free books. Simply use your login credentials for immediate access.

Table of Contents

Preface

Currently, the amount of information we are able to produce is increasing exponentially. In the past, data storage was very expensive. However, today, new technologies make it cheaper to store this information. So we are able to generate massive amounts of data, which it is also feasible to store. This means that we are immersed in a universe of data, of which we are not able to exploit the vast majority.

Among these large deposits of data storage there is valuable knowledge, but it is hidden and difficult to identify using traditional methods.

Fortunately, new technologies such as artificial intelligence, machine learning, and the management of databases converge with other disciplines that are more traditional such as statistics or mathematics to create the means to locate, extract, or even construct this valuable information from raw data.

This convergence of knowledge areas gives rise to, for example, very important subfields such as supervised learning and unsupervised learning, both derived from machine learning.

Both subfields contain a large quantity of tools to enhance the use of stored data so that it is possible to generate knowledge about the data and extract it in a human-interpretable way.

In this book, you will learn how to implement some of the most important concepts of unsupervised learning directly in the R console, one of the best tools for a data scientist, through practical examples using more than 40 R packages and a lot of useful functions.

Considering the wide range of techniques and knowledge related to unsupervised learning, this book is not intended to be in any way exhaustive. However, it contains some valuable knowledge and main techniques to introduce the reader to the study and implementation of this important sub field of machine learning.

What this book covers

Chapter 1, *Welcome to the Age of Information Technology*, aims at introducing the reader to the unsupervised learning context and explains the relation between unsupervised and supervised learning in the context of data mining. It also provides the reader with an introduction to the key concepts of information theory.

Chapter 2, *Working with Data – Exploratory Data Analysis*, is about some techniques for exploratory data analysis such as summarization, manipulation, correlation, and data visualization. An adequate knowledge of data, by exploration, is essential in order to apply unsupervised learning algorithms correctly. This assertion is true for any effort in data mining, not just for unsupervised learning.

Chapter 3, *Identifying and Understanding Groups – Clustering Algorithms*, teaches the readers about one of the most used techniques in unsupervised learning, clustering. Identifying groups can help discover and explain some patterns hidden in data. It is frequently the answer for multiple problems in many industries or contexts. Finding clusters can help uncover relationships in data, which can in turn be used to support future decisions.

Chapter 4, *Association Rules*, covers another grouping technique, the association rules. The association process makes groups of observations and attempts to discover links or associations between different attributes of groups. This association becomes rules, which can in turn be used to support future decisions.

Chapter 5, *Dimensionality Reduction*, aims to explain some dimensionality reduction techniques. In machine learning, this concept is the process of reducing the number of random variables considered, and it can be subdivided into feature selection and extraction. The key is to reduce the number of dimensions, but preserve most parts of the information.

Chapter 6, *Feature Selection Methods*, explains some techniques for feature selection, also known as variable selection or attribute selection. The key point is to choose a subset of relevant features of variables for modeling and not to use features that seem to be redundant, considering correlation to simplify model construction.

Appendix, *References*, provides a list of links referenced in the book, which are sorted chapter-wise. Given the amount of package and functions used in this book, it is very difficult to cite references and authors within the text of each chapter, as it would appear intermittent for the reader.

What you need for this book

You need to download R to follow the examples. You can download and install R using the CRAN website available at `http://cran.r-project.org/`. All the code was written using RStudio. RStudio is an integrated development environment (IDE) for R and can be downloaded from `http://www.rstudio.com/products/rstudio/`. Many of the examples are created using R packages, and they are discussed in their respective sections.

Who this book is for

This book is intended for professionals who are interested in data analysis using unsupervised learning techniques, as well as data analysts, statisticians, and data scientists seeking to learn to use R to apply data mining techniques. Knowledge of R, machine learning, and mathematics would help, but are not a strict requirement.

Conventions

In this book, you will find a number of text styles that distinguish between different kinds of information. Here are some examples of these styles and an explanation of their meaning.

Code words in text, database table names, folder names, filenames, file extensions, pathnames, dummy URLs, user input, and Twitter handles are shown as follows:

A block of code is set as follows:

```
# Clean the Work Space
rm(list = ls(all = TRUE))

# Read the iris.csv file

Iris <- read.table("iris.csv", header = TRUE,
sep = ",",dec = ".", row.names = 1)
```

In R it is a general practice to use <- for assignment instead of the = sign.

New terms and **important words** are shown in bold. Words that you see on the screen, for example in menus or dialog boxes, appear in the text like this: "We can also use the **Summary of dataset** option for exploratory data analysis:"

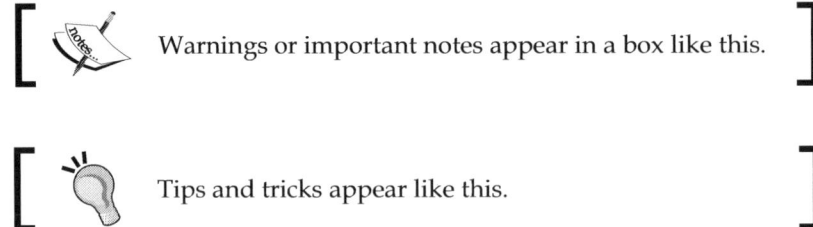

Warnings or important notes appear in a box like this.

Tips and tricks appear like this.

Reader feedback

Feedback from our readers is always welcome. Let us know what you think about this book—what you liked or disliked. Reader feedback is important for us as it helps us develop titles that you will really get the most out of.

To send us general feedback, simply e-mail feedback@packtpub.com, and mention the book's title in the subject of your message.

If there is a topic that you have expertise in and you are interested in either writing or contributing to a book, see our author guide at www.packtpub.com/authors.

Customer support

Now that you are the proud owner of a Packt book, we have a number of things to help you to get the most from your purchase.

Downloading the example code

You can download the example code files from your account at http://www.packtpub.com for all the Packt Publishing books you have purchased. If you purchased this book elsewhere, you can visit http://www.packtpub.com/support and register to have the files e-mailed directly to you.

Downloading the color images of this book

We also provide you with a PDF file that has color images of the screenshots/diagrams used in this book. The color images will help you better understand the changes in the output. You can download this file from http://www.packtpub.com/sites/default/files/downloads/1234OT_ColorImages.pdf.

Errata

Although we have taken every care to ensure the accuracy of our content, mistakes do happen. If you find a mistake in one of our books—maybe a mistake in the text or the code—we would be grateful if you could report this to us. By doing so, you can save other readers from frustration and help us improve subsequent versions of this book. If you find any errata, please report them by visiting http://www.packtpub.com/submit-errata, selecting your book, clicking on the **Errata Submission Form** link, and entering the details of your errata. Once your errata are verified, your submission will be accepted and the errata will be uploaded to our website or added to any list of existing errata under the Errata section of that title.

To view the previously submitted errata, go to https://www.packtpub.com/books/content/support and enter the name of the book in the search field. The required information will appear under the **Errata** section.

Piracy

Piracy of copyrighted material on the Internet is an ongoing problem across all media. At Packt, we take the protection of our copyright and licenses very seriously. If you come across any illegal copies of our works in any form on the Internet, please provide us with the location address or website name immediately so that we can pursue a remedy.

Please contact us at copyright@packtpub.com with a link to the suspected pirated material.

We appreciate your help in protecting our authors and our ability to bring you valuable content.

Questions

If you have a problem with any aspect of this book, you can contact us at questions@packtpub.com, and we will do our best to address the problem.

1
Welcome to the Age of Information Technology

Machine learning is one of the disciplines that is most frequently used in data mining and can be subdivided into two main tasks: supervised learning and unsupervised learning. This book will concentrate mainly on unsupervised learning.

So, let's begin this journey right from the start. This particular chapter aims to introduce you to the unsupervised learning context. We will begin by explaining the concept of data mining and mentioning the main disciplines that we use in data mining.

Next, we will provide a high-level introduction of some key concepts about information theory. Information theory studies the transmission, processing, utilization, and even extraction of information and has been successfully applied in the data mining context.

Additionally, we will introduce CRISP DM because it is important to use a specialized methodology for management knowledge discovery projects.

Finally, we will introduce the software tools that we will use in this book, mentioning some of the reasons why they are highly recommended.

In brief, we will cover the following topics:

- The data mining concepts
- Machine learning
    - Supervised learning
    - Unsupervised learning

- Information Theory
  - ◦ Entropy
  - ◦ Information gain
- CRISP-DM
- Benefits of using R

The information age

At present, the amount of data we are able to produce, transmit, and store is growing at an unprecedented rate. Within these large volumes of information, we can find deposits of valuable knowledge to be extracted. However, the main problem is to find such information and it is reasonable to say that it will become increasingly difficult.

Eric Emerson Schmidt, who was the chief executive of Google warned:

> *"Between the origin of the Earth and 2003 five Exabytes of information were created; today that amount is created every two weeks..."*

In this context, it is easy to understand that it is virtually impossible to identify these deposits of knowledge by manual methods, and this makes it necessary to resort to specialized disciplines such as data mining.

Data mining

The term began to be used in the '80s by database developers. Data mining can be defined as the process of discovery of new and meaningful relationships by exploring large volumes of information.

Data mining, as an oriented knowledge discovery process, uses various disciplines, such as mathematics, statistics, artificial intelligence, databases, pattern recognition, or machine learning. Indeed, sometimes some of these terms are considered synonymous, which is in fact incorrect. Rather, there is an overlap of these disciplines.

The following diagram illustrates some disciplines involved in the process of data mining:

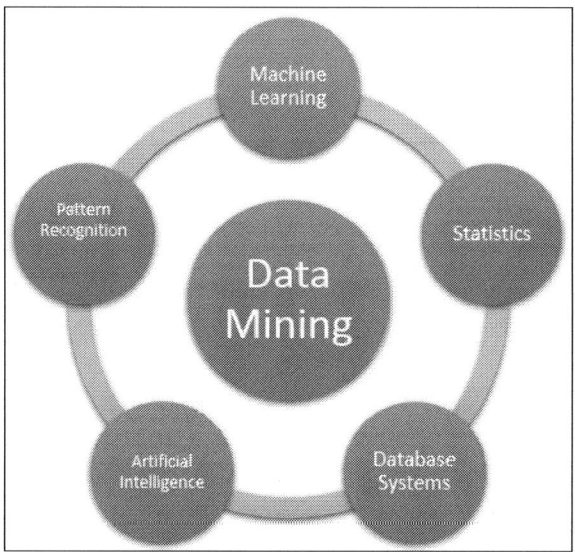

Machine learning

Machine learning is a subfield of computer science, and is defined as the study and creation of algorithms that are able to learn, in the context of this book, from the relationships between the information contained in a dataset.

In general terms, machine learning can be divided into several categories; the two most common ones are supervised learning and unsupervised learning.

Supervised learning

This is a task of machine learning, which is executed by a set of methods aimed to infer a function from the training data.

Normally, the training data is composed of a set of observations. Each observation possesses a diverse number of variables named **predictors**, and one variable that we want to predict, also known as **labels** or **classes**. These labels or classes represent the **teachers** because the models learn from them.

The ultimate aim of the function created by the model is the extrapolation of its behavior towards new observations, that is, prediction. This prediction corresponds to the output value of a supervised learning model that could be numeric, as in the case of a regression problem; or a class, as in the case of classification problems.

To explain the process of supervised learning, we can resort to the following diagram:

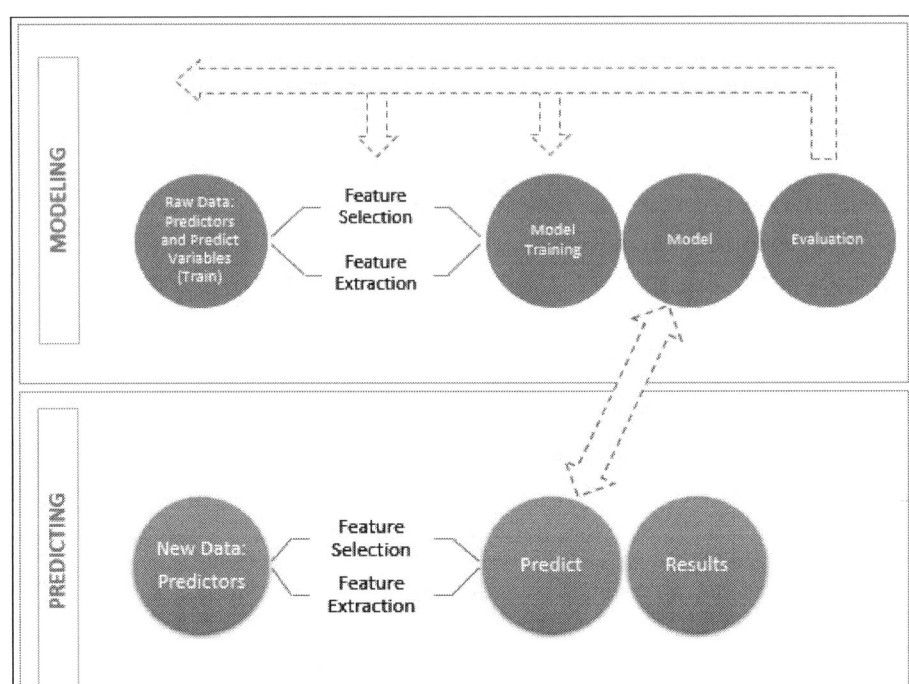

For reference, some examples of supervised learning models are:

- Regression models
- Neural networks
- Support vector machines
- Random forests
- Boosting algorithms

We can divide the process into two stages **Modeling** and **Predicting**:

In the modeling stage, we start with raw data that will be used to train the model. The following is the definition of the variables used to build the model, as it is possible to reduce the number or transform them.

We proceed to train the model, and finally carry out the evaluation. It is important to note that training, construction, and validation of the model form an iterative process aimed at achieving the best possible model, which means we may need to return to a previous step to make adjustments.

The second stage is the prediction. We already have the model and a number of new observations. Using the model that we built and tested, a prediction for new data is executed and the results are generated.

Unsupervised learning

The unsupervised learning objective of this book is a machine learning task that aims to describe the associations and patterns in relation to a set of input variables. The fundamental difference from supervised learning is that input data has no class labels, so it has no variables to predict and rather tries to find data structures by their relationship.

We could say that unsupervised learning aims to simulate the human learning process, which implies learning without explicit supervision, that is, without a *teacher* as is the case with supervised learning.

In *unsupervised learning*, we can also speak of two stages: *Modeling* and *profiting*:

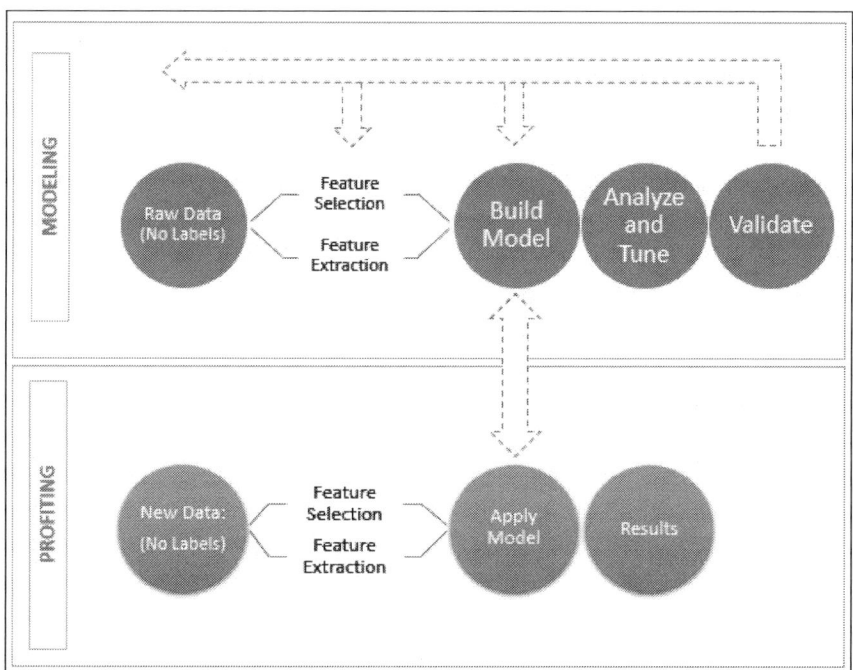

In the modeling phase, we take the input data and proceed to apply techniques of feature selection or feature extraction. Once we define the most convenient variables, we proceed to choose the best method of unsupervised learning to solve the problem at hand. For example, it could be a problem of clustering or association rules.

After choosing the method, we proceed to build the model and execute an iterative tuning process until we are satisfied with the results.

In contrast to supervised learning, in which the model value is derived mostly from prediction, in unsupervised learning, the findings obtained during the modeling phase could be enough to fulfill the purpose, in which case, the process would stop. For example, if the objective is to make a customer group, once done, the modeling phase will have an idea of the existing groups, and that could be the goal of the analysis.

Assuming that the model was subsequently used, there is a second stage, which is when we have the model and want to exploit it again. We will receive new data and use the model that we built to run on them and get results.

Throughout this book, we will explain in greater depth, many aspects of unsupervised learning.

Information theory

Information theory studies the transmission, processing, utilization, and even extraction of information and has been successfully applied in the data mining context.

Information theory, also known as the *mathematical theory of communication* or the *mathematical information theory* is a theory proposed by Claude E. Shannon and Warren Weaver in the late 1940s.

Information theory is a concept that has been extrapolated to other contexts and is widely used in relation to machine learning and unsupervised learning. Considering that in several examples of this book, some concepts will be mentioned. In this regard, we will explain them in this section.

Information theory defines the degree of dependence between two variables based on the concept of mutual information; that is, the information that is common between two variables and therefore, it can be considered a measure of the reduction of uncertainty about the value of a variable once we know the other.

In relation to the above, there are two important concepts that we want to clarify: the entropy and information gain.

Entropy

Entropy, also known as the information media, gives the mean value of the information by a variable. It can be considered a measure of uncertainty, because it is a measure of how pure or impure a variable is. The entropy ranges from 0 when all instances of a variable have the same value, to 1 when there exists an equal number of instances of each value.

Formally, the entropy can be defined with the help of the following formula:

Entropy

$$I = -\sum_{i=1}^{k} P(value_i) * log_2\big(P(value_i)\big)$$

Explaining the mathematical concepts of information theory is beyond the scope of this book. However, considering its importance, we will explain the concept of entropy and information gain using an example:

Suppose we have the following dataset consisting of four variables (**Color**, **Size**, **Shape**, and **Result**) and 16 observations:

Color	Size	Shape	Result
Y	S	R	F
G	L	I	F
G	S	R	F
Y	L	R	F
Y	L	R	F
Y	L	R	F
Y	L	R	F
Y	S	R	T
G	S	I	T
Y	L	R	T
Y	S	R	T
Y	S	R	T
Y	S	R	T
Y	L	R	T
Y	S	I	T
Y	L	I	T

16 Instances:
True = 9
False = 7

Considering it contains 16 instances: 9 TRUE and 7 FALSE, we proceed to apply the formula of entropy as follows:

$$I(Ex) = -\left[\left(\frac{9}{16}\right)log_2\left(\frac{9}{16}\right) + \left(\frac{7}{16}\right)log_2\left(\frac{7}{16}\right)\right]$$

$$I(Ex) = 0.9887$$

The entropy for the example is *0.9887*, which makes much sense because *7/16* and *9/16* is almost a coin flip; hence, the entropy is close to *1*.

Information gain

When we are trying to decide the relevance of an attribute, we can examine the information gain associated with the variable. Information gains are usually a good measure to decide the relevance of an attribute. It is a measure related to entropy and can be defined as the expected reduction in entropy caused by a partitioning of features. In general terms, the expected information gain is the change in information entropy.

We can calculate the expected entropy of each possible attribute. In other words, the degree to which the entropy would change.

Continuing with the example, we consider the variable size and proceed to the calculation of information gain.

We want to calculate the information gain (entropy reduction), that is, the reduction in uncertainty using the feature size.

The first thing to do is calculate the entropy of each subset of the variable:

Feature: Size								
	Small					Large		
Color	Size	Shape	Result		Color	Size	Shape	Result
Y	S	R	F		G	L	I	F
G	S	R	F		Y	L	R	F
Y	S	R	T		Y	L	R	F
G	S	I	T		Y	L	R	F
Y	S	R	T		Y	L	R	F
Y	S	R	T		Y	L	R	T
Y	S	R	T		Y	L	R	T
Y	S	I	T		Y	L	I	T
	True= 6 / False=2					True= 3 / False=5		

$$\frac{6}{8} \; \log_2 \left(\frac{6}{8} \right) + \frac{2}{8} \; \log_2 \left(\frac{2}{8} \right) \qquad \frac{3}{8} \; \log_2 \left(\frac{3}{8} \right) + \frac{5}{8} \; \log_2 \left(\frac{5}{8} \right)$$

Entropy(Small)= 0,811 $\qquad$ Entropy(Large)= 0,9544

Then we must add the entropies calculated according to the proportion of observations. In the example, both **Size = Small** and **Size = Large** contain eight observations:

$$I(S_{Size}) = \left(\frac{8}{16}\right) * 0.8113 + \left(\frac{8}{16}\right) * 0.9544$$

$$I(S_{Size}) = 0.8828$$

As the information gained by definition is the change from entropy:

$$IG = Entropy(S) - Entropy(S_{Size})$$
$$IG = 0.9887 - 0.8828$$
$$IG = 0.1059$$

So, we gained 0.1059 bits of information about the dataset by choosing the size feature.

Data mining methodology and software tools

To conclude this introductory chapter, we consider it important to note two additional points: a suggested methodology for data mining projects and some important aspects of the software that we use in this book.

CRISP-DM

CRISP-DM is an acronym for **Cross Industry Standard Process for Data Mining**. Although it is a process model for data mining projects in general, it is a good framework to use in *unsupervised learning* projects. It is not the only existing standard, but currently, is the most often used.

CRISP-DM, is divided into 4 levels of abstraction organized hierarchically in tasks ranging from the most general level to the most specific cases and organizes the development of a data mining project, in a series of six phases:

CRISP-DM Stages	Purpose
Business understanding	This aims to understand the project objectives and requirements from a business perspective and convert this knowledge into a data mining problem.
Data understanding	This pretends to get familiar with data, to identify quality problems, and to get first insights into the data.
Data preparation	This covers all activities to construct the final dataset to feed into the modeling tool. The data preparation phase might include tasks such as attribute selection, data transformation, data cleaning, and any other task considered necessary.
Modeling	The modeling techniques are selected, calibrated, and applied.
Evaluation	Before proceeding to the final deployment of the model, it is important to perform a more thorough evaluation, reviewing the steps executed for its construction, and to be sure it properly achieves the business objectives.
Deployment	This is the exploitation phase of the project.

These phases interact in an ordered process, as shown in the following diagram:

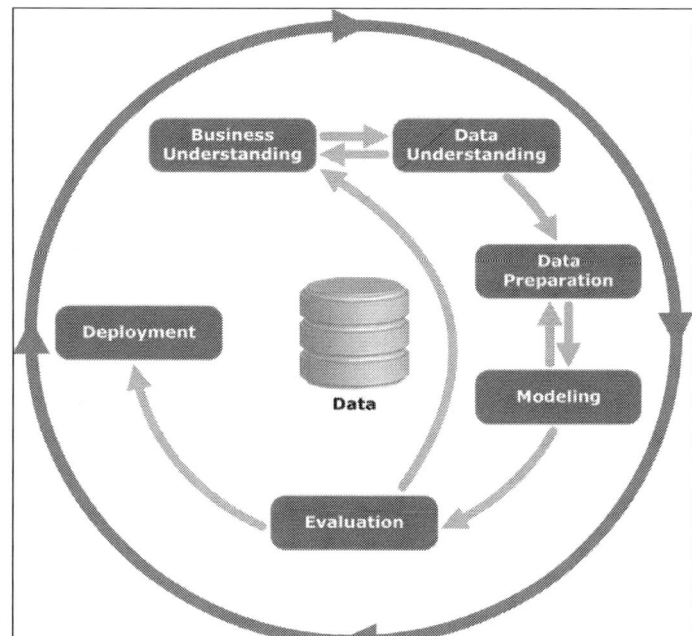

We will not delve into an explanation of each of these phases. Instead, we simply suggest the methodology as a framework. However, if you want to investigate further, there is much information available online.

Benefits of using R

This book is based entirely on the use of R—a tool that was originally developed by Robert Gentleman and Ross Ihaka from the Department of Statistics at the University of Auckland in 1993. Its current development is the responsibility of the R Development Core Team.

There are many tools for data mining, so let's take a look at a few of the benefits of using R:

- R is Free! And not just free, R is open source software.
- It is probably the most used tool for the scientific community to carry out research, and certainly the most used by professionals working in data mining.

- Perhaps one of the best features it has is a giant collaborative repository called CRAN, which currently has more than 7,300 packages for many different purposes. Very few applications have this diversity.

- It has a very active community along with multiple forums where we can discuss our queries with others and solve our problems.

- R has great capacities for information visualization.

- And a huge so on...

Summary

In this chapter, we have contextualized the concept of unsupervised learning relative to machine learning, supervised learning, and the theory of information.

In addition, we presented a methodology for data mining project management. Finally, we presented the software we plan to use throughout the chapters of this book.

In the next chapter, we will explain some exploratory techniques and thus proceed to execute the next step in the CRISP-DM methodology.

2
Working with Data – Exploratory Data Analysis

This chapter aims to explain and apply some techniques for exploratory data analysis: summarization, manipulation, correlation, and data visualization. An adequate knowledge of data by exploration is essential in order to apply unsupervised learning algorithms correctly. This asseveration is true not only for unsupervised learning but also for any efforts invested in data mining.

In the context of the methodology suggested in *Chapter 1, Welcome to the Age of Information Technology*, under the *CRISP-DM* section, once we have finalized the business understanding phase, it implies that we are clear about the context of the problem and objectives pursued. It is then that we enter the second phase — the understanding of the data — and we will do this through exploratory analysis techniques.

As we have seen in the previous chapter, R is a versatile programming language as far as data management is concerned; in this chapter, we will explain some of the potential in relation to data exploration.

In this chapter, will cover the following aspects:

- Importance of the exploratory analysis
- Loading data into R
- Basic exploration of a dataset
- Exploration of data using visualizations
- Exploring relations between data
- Exploration by end-user interfaces

Exploratory data analysis

In any project aimed at knowledge discovery, the exploratory analysis of the data should not be underestimated. It's a very important phase and it is necessary for us to dedicate a lot of time on this.

For anyone who has worked with data, the use of a methodology might help to easily understand what I mean by exploratory analysis intuitively. However, before we get to a definition, I would like to explain it with an analogy:

In an editorial process, as is the creation of this book, I develop and propose a lot of material such as: concepts, topics, examples, code, in short, plenty of information. In fact, much of this information will not be used in the published version of the book, indeed, and it is likely that the finished version of the book does not match the order in which it was developed. This would be the equivalent of raw data in a process of knowledge discovery such as unsupervised learning.

The process continues and the data enters the editing stage, in which several actors will understand, refine, and verify the consistency and presentation of them. Exploratory data analysis is what happens during the editing phase and allows us to understand the relations between variables to identify initial problems with the data and also to determine if the original data requires any transformation.

In short, the data begins to tell us a story, and to tell this story, we can make use of visualization techniques, summarization, transformation, and handling of data. In this task, the statistical techniques play an important role, as well as specialized software tools that facilitate our work.

Loading a dataset

Loading the data of the work in any tool is the first approach we will have to carry out (assuming that we don't help with the data collection phase).

Even though the exploratory analysis techniques do not require, in a strict sense, the application of computational tools, it´s reasonable to think that, in modern times, it will be used. On this basis, the first thing that we need to do is to load the data that we intend to explore in our working tool: for the purposes of this book, R for statistical computation and graphics.

This book is not intended to be an introductory course to R, and there is a lot of very good literature to learn about R. However, for your convenience, we will review some important basic aspects required to continue with this book.

Before loading the data, it is important to define a working directory according to our needs. This will allow us to work in an orderly manner and, besides, the project files will be in the place we want.

Let us proceed to upload the data to the R console:

```
# Check the current working directory
getwd()
[1] "C:/Unsupervised Learning"

# Assign the chosen working directory
setwd("C:/Unsupervised Learning/Chapter 02")

# Verifying the chosen working directory
getwd()
[1] "C:/Unsupervised Learning/Chapter 02"

# Getting the file names contained in directory
dir()
[1] "iris.csv"
```

As the reader, you will probably know, in R code, the comments are preceded by a # character. Also, when you find this character within parentheses [#], this is an indicator that the line is a result or a response to the user from the R console. In the previous example, the dir() command is an order that the user makes to the console and the console responds with [1] iris.csv. The number 1 corresponds to the line number and the phrase iris.csv is the result, in this case the name of the file found in the directory.

The Iris.csv file contains the information from a dataset widely used for learning process in statistics or data mining. It comes preloaded with R, but in order to exemplify a load of data, let's add it to the console from a comma-separated file:

```
# Clean the Work Space
rm(list = ls(all = TRUE))

# Read the iris.csv file

Iris <- read.table("iris.csv", header = TRUE, sep = ",",
    dec = ".", row.names = 1)


# verifying the object class
class(Iris)

[1] "data.frame"
```

About dataset Iris: This famous (Fisher's or Anderson's) Iris dataset gives the measurements in centimeters of the variables sepal length and width, and petal length and width, respectively, for 50 flowers from each of the three species of Iris. The species are Iris setosa, versicolor, and virginica.

At this point, we have a data frame named `Iris` loaded in R, which is merely a copy of the data that was inside the `iris.csv` file and we have loaded it using the `read.table` function.

Something very important to keep in mind is that R can load data from almost any source and file type normally used. For example, using the previous example, if the file that was just loaded was in excel format and not a comma-separated file, we could load it using the package `XL Connect`:

```
# Load or Install the library XL Connect
suppressWarnings(suppressMessages(if (!require(XLConnect))
install.packages("XLConnect")))
library("XLConnect")

# Loads or creates a Microsoft Excel workbook for
# further manipulation.
IrisXls = loadWorkbook("iris.xls")

# Reads data from worksheets of a workbook.
IrisXls = readWorksheet(IrisXls, sheet = "Sheet1")
```

Continuing to explore other data sources is beyond the scope of this book. However, we want to let you know that the connectivity of R is extensive. With just a little research and you can find excellent tutorials about it.

If you don´t want to load the dataset `iris` again from the comma-separated file, it should be sufficient to execute the next instruction in the R console, before running the examples that requires the Iris object:

```
Iris <-iris
```

Downloading the example code

You can download the example code files from your account at `http://www.packtpub.com` for all the Packt Publishing books you have purchased. If you purchased this book elsewhere, you can visit `http://www.packtpub.com/support` and register to have the files e-mailed directly to you.

Basic exploration of the dataset

At this point, we have loaded the data into the R environment. This is the first major step, but we do not know much about this data yet. We will begin to gain initial understanding through some instructions to summarize the information.

Deliberately, we have left graphic versions for a later section of the chapter. In this section, the examples that we will do to return numbers and text; which, by the way are equally important tools as compared to their graphic expressions.

As a first step, directly from the console of R, we can begin verifying the basic features of the Iris dataset that we just loaded, for example its size:

```
# Retrieve or set the dimension of an object
dim(Iris)

[1] 150    5
```

The instruction `dim (Iris)` returns the dimension of an object; in this case, it indicates that the object type `data.frame` Iris that we loaded from `iris.csv` has 150 register with 5 variables, 150 rows, and 5 columns of data.

In addition to the instruction `dim`, we may also use another function to check the size in rows and columns of the object in a separate way, that is, by counting the number of rows and number of columns:

```
#nrow and ncol return the number of rows or columns

nrow(Iris)
[1] 150

ncol(Iris)
[1] 5
```

This can help us in dimensioning the size and shape of the dataset, which are the two important aspects for us to determine how manageable it will be and how we can handle it.

This is the first approach but we need more information.

In order to move forward in the exploration, we can review its structure in more detail by using another function, str():

```
# Compactly Display the Structure of an Arbitrary R Object

str(Iris)

# The next block of code is a console response to str
 'data.frame': 150 obs. of  5 variables:

$ Sepal.Length: num 5.1 4.9 4.7 4.6 5 5.4 4.6 5 4.4 4.9 ...
$ Sepal.Width : num 3.5 3 3.2 3.1 3.6 3.9 3.4 3.4 2.9 3.1...
$ Petal.Length: num 1.4 1.4 1.3 1.5 1.4 1.7 1.4 1.5 1.4 1.5...
$ Petal.Width : num 0.2 0.2 0.2 0.2 0.2 0.4 0.3 0.2 0.2 0.1...
$ Species : Factor w/ 3 levels "setosa","versicolor",..: 1
    1 1 1 1 1 1 1 1 ...
```

This instruction gives us additional information about the structure of the Iris object, for example:

We can verify that Iris is an object of type data.frame, which has 150 observations with 5 variables each, and which also shows us the names of those variables and (something to which we must pay close attention now) the data type that stores each variable.

At this point, we have a better knowledge of the loaded data from Iris.csv, and also, if we pay attention to the data type for each variable, we can determine whether any error has occurred in the information loading. Considering that the variables Sepal.Length, Sepal.Width, Petal.Length, Petal.Width correspond to measurements in centimeters, we know their type must be numeric or num as reflected in the str function.

Considering this type of error happens frequently, we will simulate an incorrect loading of data to allow you to be clear about how you can notice and correct this problem in the early stages of exploration.

We will reload the iris.csv data file wrongly, using the following instruction:

```
# Read incorrectly the iris.csv file

BadIris <- read.table("iris.csv", header = TRUE, sep = ",",
    dec = ",", row.names = 1)

class(BadIris)
```

Notice that the code we're using is almost identical to the original code that we used earlier to read and load data to data.frame Iris. However, if you observe carefully, we have mistaken (on purpose) the decimal separator dec = "," indicating a comma instead of a decimal point as would have been correct:

```
# Compactly Display the Structure of an Arbitrary R Object

str(BadIris)

  'data.frame': 150 obs. of  5 variables:
  $ Sepal.Length: Factor w/ 35 levels "4.3","4.4","4.5" ...
  $ Sepal.Width : Factor w/ 23 levels "2","2.2","2.3",...
  $ Petal.Length: Factor w/ 43 levels "1","1.1","1.2",..
  $ Petal.Width : Factor w/ 22 levels "0.1","0.2","0.3",...
  $ Species     : Factor w/ 3 levels "setosa","versicolor",..: 1 1 1 1
  1 1 1 1 1 ...
```

Everything looks very similar. We have a data frame of 150 observations with 5 variables each, whose names are Sepal.Length, Sepal.Width, Petal.Length, Petal.Width. However, we actually simulated making a mistake, using an incorrect decimal separator in the instruction for the data load.

As you may have noticed, the data types of variables have changed, even though we know that these variables store information about measurements in centimeters, the instruction str(BadIris) indicates that the data type of those variables is Factor, the type assigned to indicate that the stored data corresponds to a qualitative variable.

In short, although the data looks structurally similar and looks like numbers at first sight, the data type is the best indicator to verify it, and in this example, the type of the loaded data does not match what is expected from the Iris dataset.

If it had not been a simulated mistake, at this point, the right decision would be to reload the data, correcting the problem of the decimal separator and verifying through the str function that data types associated to the variables correspond to the numeric type, since any exploration that we could do about them in their current status would be useless.

 Considering its efficiency, the str() command is very safe to use, although we are working with a very large dataset.

We will return to our example with data properly loaded in the data.frame Iris.

When we have reviewed the structure of the data, it may be valuable to see how it behaves with regards to the initial portion and the final portion.

The first look at the values could help us to know whether the data was loaded properly or whether it has obvious problems, and for this we will use the functions head and tail:

```
# head returns the first parts of a vector, matrix, table,
# data frame or function

head(Iris[1:4],5)

   Sepal.Length Sepal.Width Petal.Length Petal.Width
1           5.1         3.5          1.4         0.2
2           4.9         3.0          1.4         0.2
3           4.7         3.2          1.3         0.2
4           4.6         3.1          1.5         0.2
5           5.0         3.6          1.4         0.2


# tail returns the last parts of a vector, matrix, table,
# data frame or function

tail(Iris[1:4],5)

     Sepal.Length Sepal.Width Petal.Length Petal.Width
146           6.7         3.0          5.2         2.3
147           6.3         2.5          5.0         1.9
148           6.5         3.0          5.2         2.0
149           6.2         3.4          5.4         2.3
150           5.9         3.0          5.1         1.8
```

The instructions head and tail can receive as parameters the amount of lines above or below the dataset that we want to see. In our example we have used five lines.

Notice also that through the instruction Iris [1: 4] we are indicating to R that we only require rows 1 to 4 to be displayed, namely, numeric variables.

This consideration does not relate only to the use of functions head or tail. We only want to show that they can use portions of the dataset as required, while both arguments are completely optional.

Apparently, there is no data problem, considering there are no information with unexpected formats either at the beginning or the final.

Also, we can see that apparently, the variables possess appropriate types according the `str` function, we can conclude that the data was well loaded and at least has no visible impurities, and we also have a visual idea of the form and content of the dataset.

Another important aspect that we recommend is to explore the recount, for example, Setosa = 50 and versicolor = 50. This will give us an idea of whether they are missing observations, assuming, of course, that we are aware of the number of observations that should have our working dataset. In our case, we know that the `Iris` data should have 50 observations of each type and it is something that should be validated.

To make this validation, it is possible to use the `table()` function to build a table quickly:

```
#"table" uses the cross-classifying factors to build a contingency
table of the counts at each combination of factor levels

names(Iris) # Return the columns Names for Information

[1] "Sepal.Length" "Sepal.Width"  "Petal.Length"
[4] "Petal.Width"  "Species"

table(Iris$Species) # Build the table

setosa versicolor   virginica
50          50          50
```

The preceding table indicates that the dataset has 50 plants from each of three types of flower, a total of 150 observations, which matches what we knew previously about the Iris dataset. If this is not the case and the table had a different distribution of observations, there is a high probability we would have a loading data error or an error in the file source of the information, the `iris.csv`.

The previous example may seem very simple and could lead you to undervalue the usefulness of the `table()` function. Suppose we are interested in a table with the frequency of the `Sepal.Width` variable, you could use the following instruction to set up:

```
# Return the columns Names for reference
names(Iris)

[1] "Sepal.Length" "Sepal.Width"  "Petal.Length" "Petal.Width"
"Species"

# Build the table grouping observations by sepal width
as.data.frame(table(Iris$Sepal.Width))
```

```
     Var1 Freq
1       2    1
2     2.2    3
3     2.3    4
4     2.4    3
5     2.5    8
6     2.6    5
7     2.7    9
8     2.8   14
9     2.9   10
10      3   26
11    3.1   11
12    3.2   13
13    3.3    6
14    3.4   12
15    3.5    6
```

This table corresponds to a frequency table that groups the observations according to the amount of centimeters in `Sepal.Width` and gives us information for better understanding of the dataset.

For example, we can see that there is a higher density of observations between `2.8` and `3.2` cm in relation to the lower grades.

 The use of the `as.data.frame` instruction is not indispensable. In the example, it is used to force the result to behave as an object of type `data.frame`, which has the advantage that the resulting grids are displayed vertically.

Continuing with the exploration of the Iris dataset, we can use other functions to meet the distribution and position of the data that is in it. To do this, there is a very interesting function called `summary`:

```
# Generic function used to produce result summaries of the
# results of various model fitting functions

summary(Iris)

     Sepal.Length      Sepal.Width       Petal.Length
 Min.    :4.300    Min.    :2.000    Min.    :1.000
 1st Qu.:5.100    1st Qu.:2.800    1st Qu.:1.600
 Median :5.800    Median :3.000    Median :4.350
 Mean    :5.843    Mean    :3.057    Mean    :3.758
 3rd Qu.:6.400    3rd Qu.:3.300    3rd Qu.:5.100
```

```
    Max.   :7.900   Max.    :4.400   Max.    :6.900

    Petal.Width            Species
    Min.   :0.100   setosa    :50
    1st Qu.:0.300   versicolor:50
    Median :1.300   virginica :50
    Mean   :1.199
    3rd Qu.:1.800
    Max.   :2.500
```

This function displays important information about the distribution of data. In the case of the numeric variables, it details the minimum value, maximum value, the arithmetic mean, the first and third quartiles, the median, and implicitly interquartile range. In the case of qualitative variables or factors, as is the case of the species variable, the function shows a count for each of the available categories or factors.

Now, we can say that we know the Iris dataset better, but if we go a little beyond the basic R package, we could use some very interesting libraries for that additional important information for exploration, or, at least, to represent other forms of summarization of the information. For example:

The package Hmisc contains many functions useful for data analysis, high-level graphics, utility operations, functions for computing sample size and power, importing and annotating datasets, imputing missing values, advanced table making, variable clustering, character string manipulation, conversion of R objects to LaTeX code, and recoding variables.

The following is an example using the Hmisc package:

```
# describe" determines whether the variable type
# and prints a concise statistical summary
# according to each.

suppressWarnings(
        suppressMessages(if
suppressWarnings(suppressMessages(if (!require(Hmisc))
install.packages("Hmisc")))
library("Hmisc")

describe(Iris)
```

The output will be as follows:

```
 5  Variables      150  Observations
--------------------------------------------------------------------------------
Sepal.Length
      n missing  unique     Info    Mean     .05     .10     .25     .50     .75     .90     .95
    150        0      35       1    5.843   4.600   4.800   5.100   5.800   6.400   6.900   7.255

lowest : 4.3 4.4 4.5 4.6 4.7, highest: 7.3 7.4 7.6 7.7 7.9
--------------------------------------------------------------------------------
Sepal.width
      n missing  unique     Info    Mean     .05     .10     .25     .50     .75     .90     .95
    150        0      23    0.99    3.057   2.345   2.500   2.800   3.000   3.300   3.610   3.800

lowest : 2.0 2.2 2.3 2.4 2.5, highest: 3.9 4.0 4.1 4.2 4.4
--------------------------------------------------------------------------------
Petal.Length
      n missing  unique     Info    Mean     .05     .10     .25     .50     .75     .90     .95
    150        0      43       1    3.758   1.30    1.40    1.60    4.35    5.10    5.80    6.10

lowest : 1.0 1.1 1.2 1.3 1.4, highest: 6.3 6.4 6.6 6.7 6.9
--------------------------------------------------------------------------------
Petal.width
      n missing  unique     Info    Mean     .05     .10     .25     .50     .75     .90     .95
    150        0      22    0.99    1.199   0.2     0.2     0.3     1.3     1.8     2.2     2.3

lowest : 0.1 0.2 0.3 0.4 0.5, highest: 2.1 2.2 2.3 2.4 2.5
--------------------------------------------------------------------------------
Species
      n missing  unique
    150        0       3

setosa (50, 33%), versicolor (50, 33%), virginica (50, 33%)
--------------------------------------------------------------------------------
```

This function returns a table with information for each variable. In the example shown, describe() for numeric variables, shows the recount of observations, the number of null values, the amount of unique values, the five lower values, the five highest values, the mean, median and percentile 5, 10, 25, 50, 75, 90, 95th. In the case of qualitative variables, for example the variable species, the function showing the number of missing values, the number of unique values, the overall count, and the percentage distribution for each factor.

Another very useful function for generating numerical data summarization is basicStats. We need to install the package fBasics. The following is an example on R console:

```
# "fBasics" Returns a data frame with the following entries and
row names: nobs, NAs, Minimum, Maximum , 1. Quartile, 3. Quartile,
Mean, Median, Sum, SE Mean, LCL Mean, UCL Mean, Variance, Stdev,
Skewness, Kurtosis.

# Load or install the package
suppressWarnings(
        suppressMessages(if
                        (!require(fBasics))
                        install.packages("fBasics")))
```

```
library("fBasics")
# Apply the function to all variables
 lapply(Iris[1:4][,c(1:4)], basicStats)
$Sepal.Length
                  X...X.i
nobs          150.000000
NAs             0.000000
Minimum         4.300000
Maximum         7.900000
1. Quartile     5.100000
3. Quartile     6.400000
Mean            5.843333
Median          5.800000
Sum           876.500000
SE Mean         0.067611
LCL Mean        5.709732
UCL Mean        5.976934
Variance        0.685694
Stdev           0.828066
Skewness        0.308641
Kurtosis       -0.605813
$Sepal.Width
                  X...X.i
nobs          150.000000
NAs             0.000000
Minimum         2.000000
Maximum         4.400000
1. Quartile     2.800000
3. Quartile     3.300000
Mean            3.057333
Median          3.000000
Sum           458.600000
SE Mean         0.035588
LCL Mean        2.987010
UCL Mean        3.127656
Variance        0.189979
Stdev           0.435866
Skewness        0.312615
Kurtosis        0.138705
```

To conclude with the summarization functions, we can make use of the stat.desc() function of the pastecs library:

```
#stat.desc Compute a table giving various descriptive statistics
about the variables in a data frame
suppressWarnings(
        suppressMessages(if
                        (!require(pastecs))
                        install.packages("pastecs")))
```

```
library("pastecs")

stat.desc(Iris[1:4])
```

The output will be as follows:

	Sepal.Length	Sepal.Width	Petal.Length	Petal.Width
nbr.val	150.00000000	150.00000000	150.0000000	150.00000000
nbr.null	0.00000000	0.00000000	0.0000000	0.00000000
nbr.na	0.00000000	0.00000000	0.0000000	0.00000000
min	4.30000000	2.00000000	1.0000000	0.10000000
max	7.90000000	4.40000000	6.9000000	2.50000000
range	3.60000000	2.40000000	5.9000000	2.40000000
sum	876.50000000	458.60000000	563.7000000	179.90000000
median	5.80000000	3.00000000	4.3500000	1.30000000
mean	5.84333333	3.05733333	3.7580000	1.19933333
SE.mean	0.06761132	0.03558833	0.1441360	0.06223645
CI.mean.0.95	0.13360085	0.07032302	0.2848146	0.12298004
var	0.68569351	0.18997942	3.1162779	0.58100626
std.dev	0.82806613	0.43586628	1.7652982	0.76223767
coef.var	0.14171126	0.14256420	0.4697441	0.63555114

The package `stat.desc` returns some basic statistics:

The number of values (`nbr.val`), the number of null values (`nbr.null`), the number of missing values (`nbr.na`), the minimal value (`min`), the maximum value (`max`), the range (range, that is, max-min), and the sum of all non-missing values (`sum`).

Additionally, it returns various descriptive statistics: the median (`median`), the mean (`mean`), the standard error (`SE.mean`), the confidence interval (`CI.mean`), the variance (`var`), the standard deviation (`std.dev`), and the variation coefficient (`coef.var`).

Exploring data by basic visualization

In the first part of this chapter, we covered some functions in R to perform exploratory data analysis. However, as you will have noticed, we did not cover the graphic mode topic. Graphical analysis is very important because most people understand information better with the help of a layout display.

It is important to differentiate between exploratory and final visualizations. The first ones are usually simple graphics and are made very quickly. Generally, they are created for our own understanding about information. On the other hand, the final visualizations are those that are constructed for presentation and thus take much more work and details

For exploratory visualizations, the base module of R is usually enough, while for final visualizations, we could take advantage of specialized packages like ggplot2 or lattice.

Histograms

A histogram is a graphical representation of the distribution of a numeric variable and a very useful chart when you want to observe and try to understand the full distribution of the data. The information is displayed in the form of bars, where the surface of each bar is proportionate to the frequency of the values represented.

In R, we can build a histogram as follows:

```
# Set an array of two plots in one column
par(mfrow = c(2, 1), mar = c(4, 4, 2, 1))

# Build a Histogram of Sepal.Length
hist(Iris$Sepal.Length)

# Build the same Histogram but setting brakes to 50
hist(Iris$Sepal.Length,breaks=50)
```

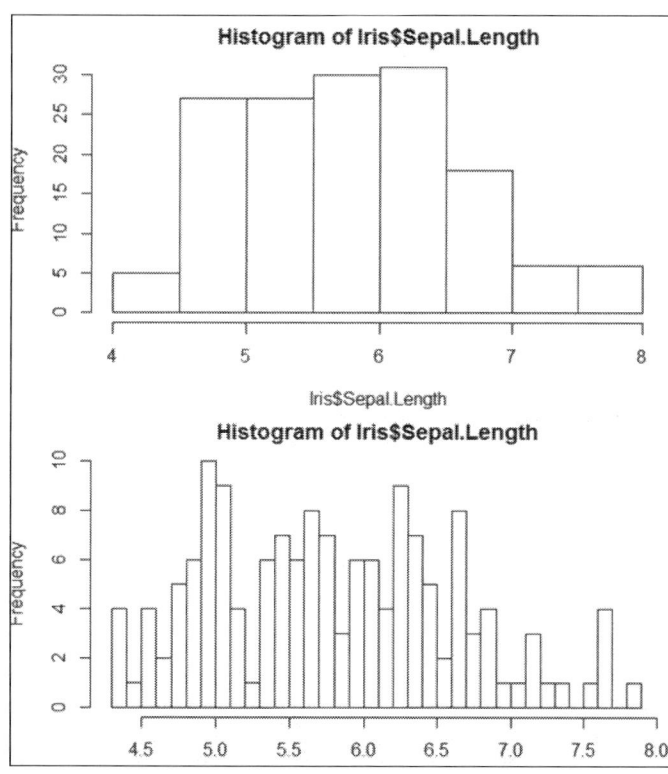

By default, the `hist` function automatically sets the number of categories or bars, in the histogram, depending on the density of the data. However, if you wish to modify that feature, you can use the parameter `breaks`, as we did in the previous example.

R is very powerful with regard to the manipulation that can be carried out in the graphs we build. For example, in the preceding histogram, it could be sufficient for an exploration graphic, however, it may not be adequate for a final graph.

For example, the following is a better version of the previous histogram:

```
par(mfrow = c(1, 1), mar = c(4, 4, 2, 1))
# Prepare data
x <- rbind(data.frame(dat = Iris[, ][, "Sepal.Length"],
    grp = "All"))

# Build a basic histogram
hs <- hist(x[x$grp == "All", 1], main = "", xlab = "Sepal.Length",
    ylab = "Frequency", col = "grey90", ylim = c(0,
        31), breaks = "fd", border = TRUE)

# Plot a density function
dens <- density(x[x$grp == "All", 1], na.rm = TRUE)
y <- max(hs$counts)/max(dens$y)
lines(dens$x, dens$y * y, type = "l", col = colorspace::rainbow_hcl(3)
[3])

# Adding a Rug to histogram
rug(x[x$grp == "All", 1])

# Adding a Title
title(main = "Distribution of Sepal Length", sub = paste("Unsupervised
Learning",
    format(Sys.time(), "%Y-%b-%d")))
```

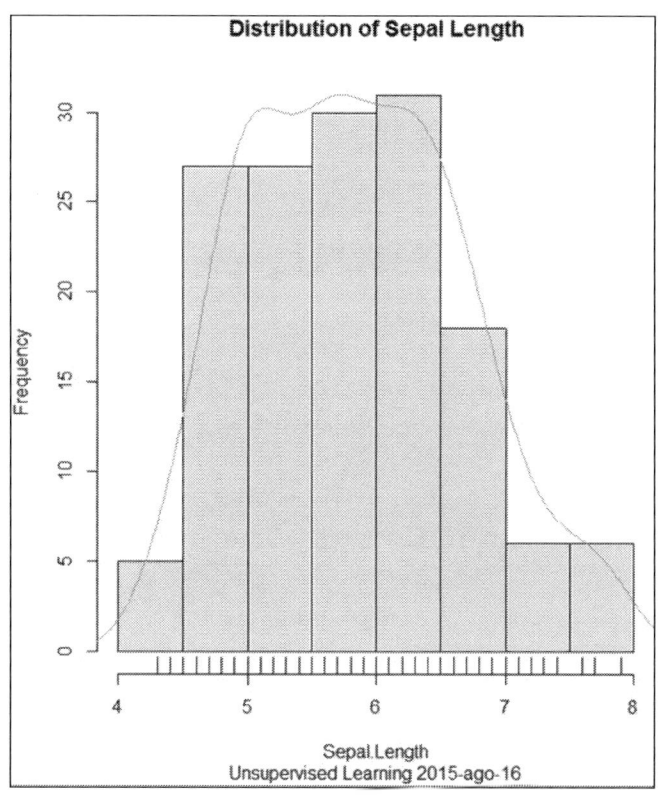

Even better, we can use a specialized package for achieving better quality, which is important if we make a final graphic, for example:

```
#Load or install the packages ggplot2 and dplyr

suppressWarnings(suppressMessages(if (!require(ggplot2))
install.packages("ggplot2")))
suppressWarnings(suppressMessages(if (!require(dplyr))
install.packages("dplyr")))
library("ggplot2")
library("dplyr")

#Prepare inputs for the histogram
x <- range(with(Iris, select(Iris[, ], Sepal.Length)))
y <- (x[2] - x[1])/nclass.FD(with(Iris, Iris[,
    ]$Sepal.Length))
```

```
#Build the histogram

object <- ggplot(with(Iris, select(Iris[,
    ], Sepal.Length, Species)), aes(x = Sepal.Length)) +
    geom_histogram(aes(y = ..density..),
        binwidth = y, fill = "grey", colour = "black") +
    geom_density(aes(colour = Species)) +
    xlab("Sepal.Length") + ggtitle("Distribution of Sepal.Length\nby
Species") +
    labs(colour = "", y = "Density")

#Print de object
print(object)
```

Using these libraries we can get a much better graphic finish, but, besides that, it is considered good practice to show comparisons. In the following chart, a histogram is constructed, but all three types are compared in relation to the plotted variable, in this case Sepal.Length:

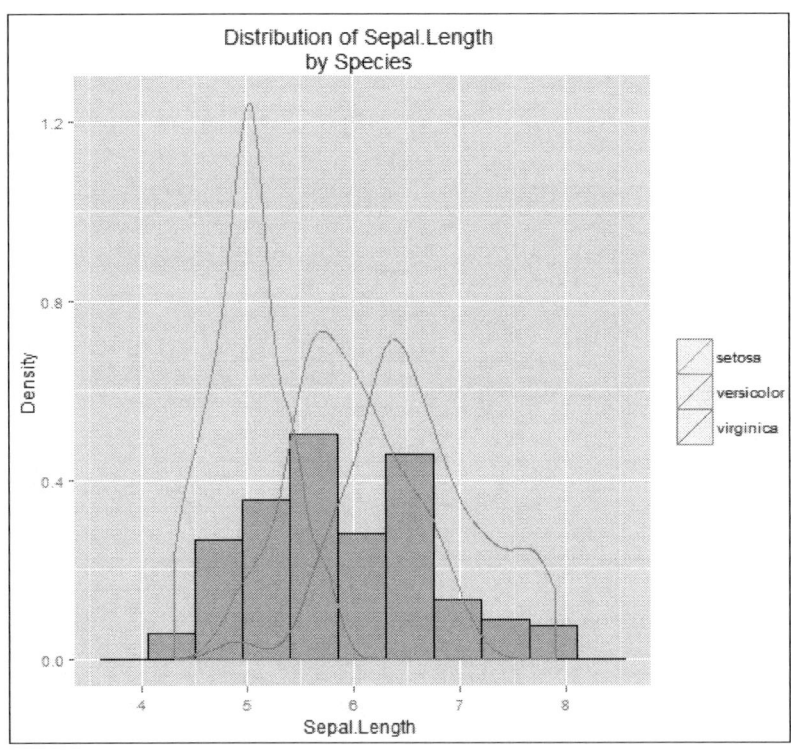

Barplots

Bar charts are used to perform <u>simple comparisons</u>; for example, they are useful to represent <u>categorical data.</u> As in the histogram, the length of the bars is proportional to the variable data being represented.

In the following example, we will alter the size of the working set data to appreciate a difference between the bars.

In the console of R, we can build a bar graph as follows:

```
# This section of code changes the size of the Iris
# dataset only.
# This is done by a sample

to obtain reproducible results
set.seed(42)

# Making sample
nobs <- nrow(Iris)  # 150 observations
sample <- train <- sample(nrow(Iris), 0.7 * nobs)  # 105 observations
Iris.Sample <- (Iris[sample, ])

# Load or install the gplots package
suppressWarnings(suppressMessages(if (!require(gplots)) install.
packages("gplots")))
library("gplots")

# Preparing data
x <- rbind(summary(na.omit(Iris.Sample$Species)))
ord <- order(x[1, ], decreasing = TRUE)

# Build the barplot
bp <- barplot2(x[, ord], beside = TRUE, ylab = "Frequency",
    xlab = "Species", ylim = c(0, 44), col = colorspace::rainbow_
hcl(4))
text(bp, x[, ord] + 3, x[, ord])
```

```
# Adding a title
title(main = "Distribution of Species (Sample)")
```

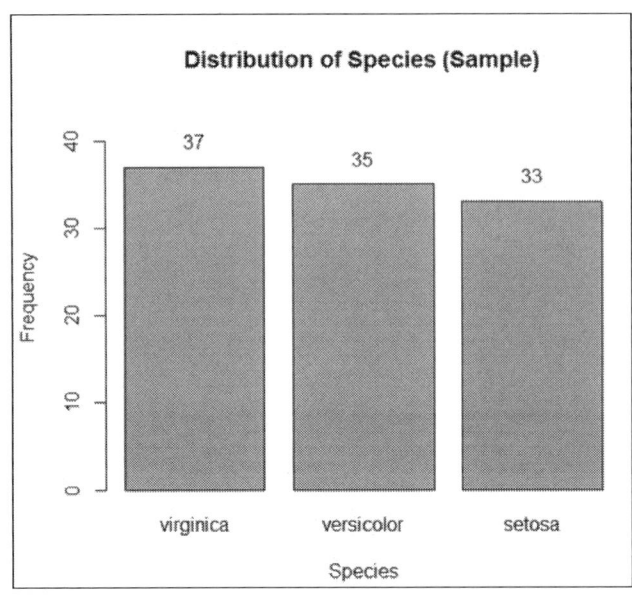

Boxplots

Boxplots are representations based on quartiles, like the histogram, and their function is to display a set of data. They consist of a rectangle (box) and two arms (whiskers).

Boxplots provide information about the minimum values, maximum values, quartiles, the distribution skewness, and, very importantly, the existence of outliers in the distribution.

An outlier is an observation point that is remote from other observations. If Q1 and Q3 are the lower and upper quartiles, respectively, then we can define an outlier to be any observation outside the range:

$$[Q_1 - k * (Q_{3-}Q_1), Q_3 + k * (Q_{3-}Q_1)]$$

Where *k* is a non-negative constant, generally *k= 1.5* is used for a slight atypical and *k=3* is used for get an extreme atypical.

We can create a boxplot in R as follows:

```
# Build the boxplot from Sepal.Length by species

boxplot(Sepal.Length ~ Species, data = Iris, ylab = "Sepal Length
(cm)",main = "Iris Data Set", boxwex = 0.5, col = colorspace::rainbow_
hcl(4))
```

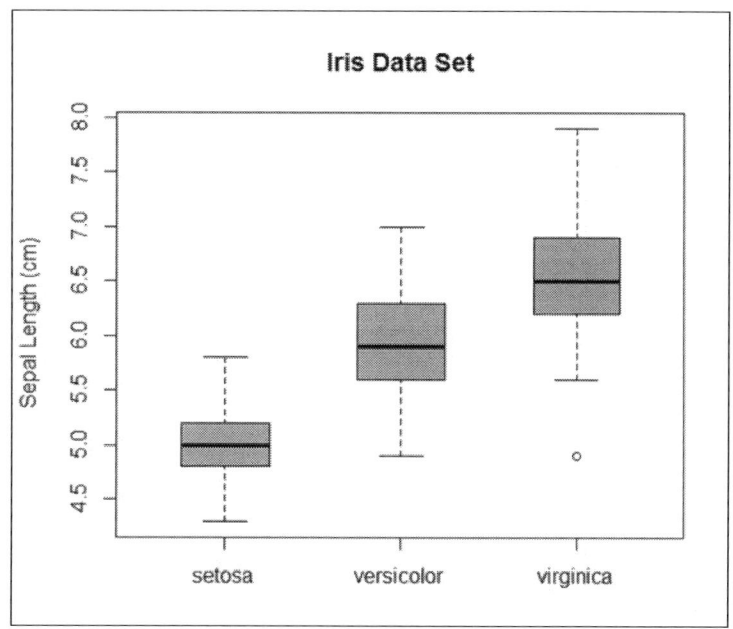

In the preceding chart, we can see a lower outlier in `virginica` plant type. However, the chart itself does not show us the detail of outlier, only its representation in the plane.

With the following trick, we can draw observations on the outliers:

```
# Load or install the package car
suppressWarnings(suppressMessages(if (!require(car))
install.packages("car")))
library("car")

# Identify the Outliers and save them in object
# named Outliers
Outliers <- (Boxplot(Sepal.Length ~ Species, data = Iris,
    id.method = "y", col = colorspace::rainbow_hcl(4)))
```

```
# Consult the outliers detected
Outliers
[1] "107"


Iris[Outliers,1:4]

    Sepal.Length Sepal.Width Petal.Length Petal.Width
107          4.9         2.5          4.5         1.7
```

As can be observed, the outlier is located on the observation identified by number 107 in the dataset, whose value is 4.9 for `Sepal.Length`.

If you want to check it, we can separate, in the data, which observations correspond to the `virginica` species and generate a summary:

```
# Subset the data set by species= Virginica

virginica<-Iris[which(Iris$Species=='virginica'),]

# Summarization by Sepal.Length

summary(virginica$Sepal.Length)

   Min. 1st Qu.  Median    Mean 3rd Qu.    Max.
  4.900   6.225   6.500   6.588   6.900   7.900
```

The value found in row 107 corresponds to an outlier because in this type of plant, these variable values are much higher, in fact `4.9` is the minimum value.

Finally, if we want to generate a boxplot for filing a final chart, with more quality finishing, we can use the `ggplot2` library:

```
# Load or install the package ggplot2

suppressWarnings(suppressMessages(if (!require(ggplot2)) install.
packages("ggplot2")))
library("ggplot2")


# Build the Box Plot for Sepal.Width

p <- ggplot(with(Iris, Iris[, ]), aes(y = Sepal.Width))
p <- p + geom_boxplot(aes(x = "All"), notch = TRUE,
    fill = "grey")
p <- p + stat_summary(aes(x = "All"), fun.y = mean,
```

```
        geom = "point", shape = 8)
p <- p + geom_boxplot(aes(x = Species, fill = Species),
    notch = TRUE)
p <- p + stat_summary(aes(x = Species), fun.y = mean,
    geom = "point", shape = 8)
p <- p + xlab("Species\n\nUnsupervised Learning")
p <- p + ggtitle("Distribution of Sepal.Width\nby Species")
p <- p + theme(legend.position = "none")
print(p)
```

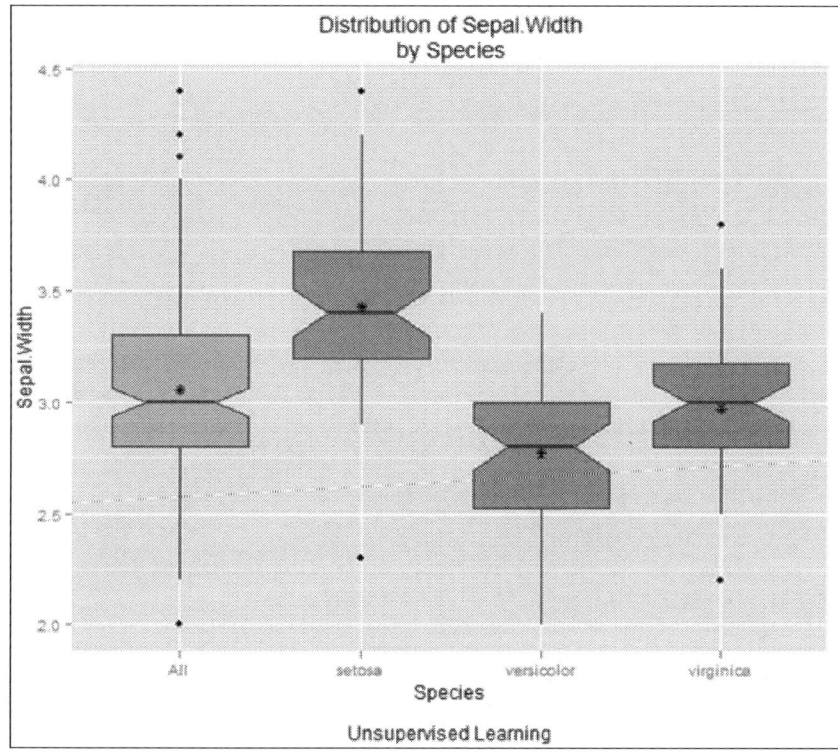

Special visualizations

This is not a book about visualizations. However, visualizations are an indispensable tool for exploratory analysis, which, itself, is an essential stage in a process of unsupervised learning.

Given the above, it is considered important to at least introduce a library that will be very useful for both kinds of visualizations: the exploration plots used in the exploration phase and for the final plots used in the presentation of results, the `lattice` library.

To make it easy for you, determine the lattice potential. We will work in this example with a different dataset that comes with R, the state.x77 dataset:

```
# "state.x77" = matrix with 50 rows and 8 columns
# giving some # statistics in the respective
# columns.  In this example:

# Income: per capita income (1974) and HS Grad:
# percent high-# school graduates (1970)

# Clean the environment for work
rm(list = ls(all = TRUE))

# Load or install the package lattice
suppressWarnings(suppressMessages(if (!require(lattice))
install.packages("lattice")))
library("lattice")
# Build a data frame from state.x77 adding
# state.name and state.region columns
state <- data.frame(state.x77, state.name =
dimnames(state.x77)[[1]],
    state.region = state.region)
# Check the head of data set
head(state)
# Build the XY Plot by HS.Grad and Income grouping by state
xyplot(HS.Grad ~ Income | state.region, data = state,
    groups = state.name, panel = function(x, y, subscripts,
        groups) ltext(x = x, y = y, label = groups[subscripts],
        cex = 1, fontfamily = "HersheySans"))
```

This graphic is very interesting because it allows us to relate two variables separately for four regions, and locate the name of the state in the corresponding quadrant, which summarizes a lot of information. Furthermore, the level of the visual quality of the lattice library allows us to use it to build exploratory visualizations or to build final visualizations.

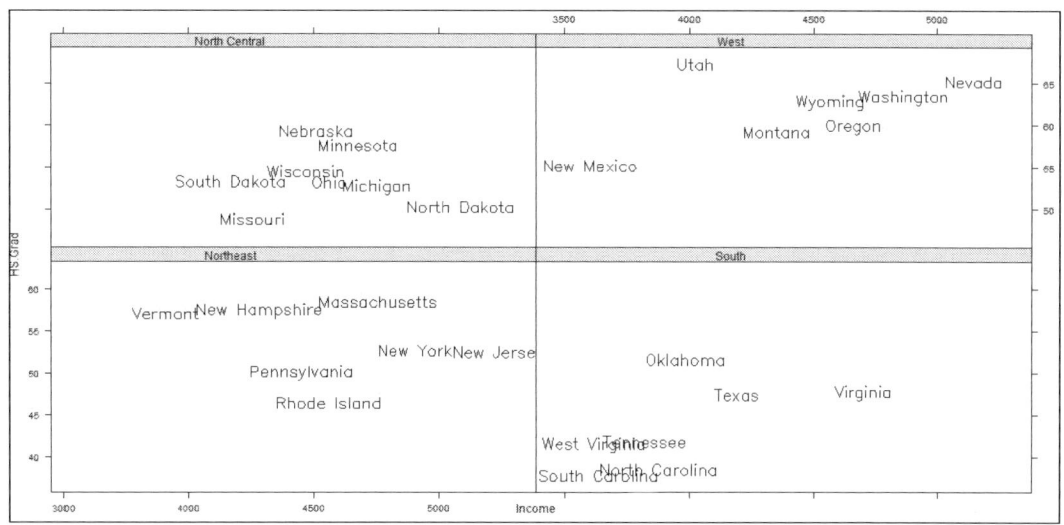

In addition to the large number of options contained in the `lattice` library, we can also use a resource base package R. It could be be interesting to build Scatterplot Matrices, as long as the dataset is not too complex.

```
#A matrix of scatterplots is produced

pairs(Iris[1:3], main = "Anderson's Iris Data -- 3 species",
pch = c(21),   cex = 2,bg = c("red","green3","blue")
[unclass(iris$Species)])
```

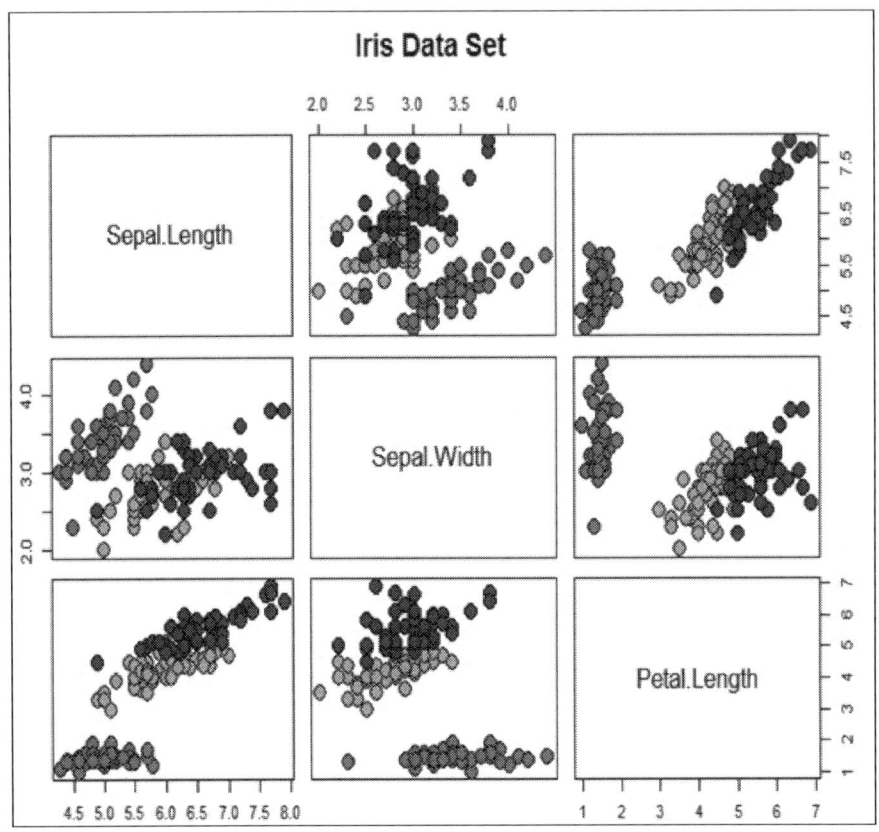

This graphics array can be interesting because it compares, at the same time, the behavior of all the combinations of variables separately for each type of observation.

Exploring relations in data

Analyzing the correlation between variables is a fundamental aspect in the exploration phase. We need to consider that many models necessarily assume independence of variables and determine the magnitude and direction in which they relate.

The correlation is a statistical technique that aims to indicate the strength and direction of the relationship between two variables, determining whether one systematically varies depending on the other.

R has functions for calculating a correlation matrix between variables:

```
# Create the data.frame Iris
data(iris)
Iris<-iris

# Load or Install the library Ellipse
suppressWarnings(suppressMessages(if (!require(ellipse)) install.
packages("ellipse")))
library("ellipse")

# Build the correlations Matrix
corr <- cor(Iris[, -5])

# Print the correlations Matrix
corr
             Sepal.Length Sepal.Width Petal.Length Petal.Width
Sepal.Length    1.0000000  -0.1175698    0.8717538   0.8179411
Sepal.Width    -0.1175698   1.0000000   -0.4284401  -0.3661259
Petal.Length    0.8717538  -0.4284401    1.0000000   0.9628654
Petal.Width     0.8179411  -0.3661259    0.9628654   1.0000000
```

 Note that the correlation coefficient varies between –1 and 1, wherein the first implies a perfect inverse correlation and the second a perfect direct correlation.

About their interpretation, the diagonal of the matrix is always 1 because that is where each variable row intersects with mirror columns.

Each variable in the rows that are calculated correlate with the variables in the columns. For example, if we need to know the correlation between Petal.Width and Petal.Length, we have to look at the intersection row 4 and column 4 of the table, storing a correlation of 0.9628654, implying a very high positive correlation.

In the Iris dataset, as you would expect, there are strong correlations.

Analyzing the correlation table is interesting but, it is also possible, and sometimes very useful, to work with a graphic expression, for example:

```
# Load or install the library ellipse
suppressWarnings(suppressMessages(if (!require(ellipse)) install.
packages("ellipse")))
library("ellipse")

# Build the correlations Matrix
corr <- cor(Iris[, 1:4])

# Colour the ellipses to emphasize the differences.
colors <- c("#A50F15", "#DE2D26", "#FB6A4A", "#FCAE91",
    "#FEE5D9", "white", "#EFF3FF", "#BDD7E7", "#6BAED6",
    "#3182BD", "#08519C")

# Plot the correlation matrix by ellipses
plotcorr(corr, col = colors)
```

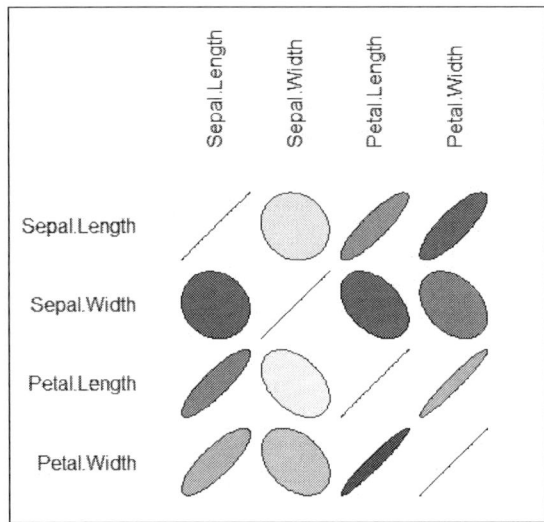

The `plotcorr` function plots a correlation matrix using ellipse-shaped glyphs for each entry. The ellipse represents a level curve of the density of a bivariate normal with the matching correlation.

You can also use the library `corrplot`, which is personally my favorite, because it has many options for displaying correlation matrices:

```
# Load or install the package corrplot

suppressWarnings(suppressMessages(if (!require(corrplot)) install.
packages("corrplot")))
library("corrplot")

# Set a color Palette

col <- colorRampPalette(c("#BB4444", "#EE9988", "#FFFFFF",
    "#77AADD", "#4477AA"))

# Plot the correlation Matrix
corrplot(corr, method = "pie", shade.col = NA, tl.col = "black",
    tl.srt = 45, col = col(200), addCoef.col = "black",
    order = "AOE")
```

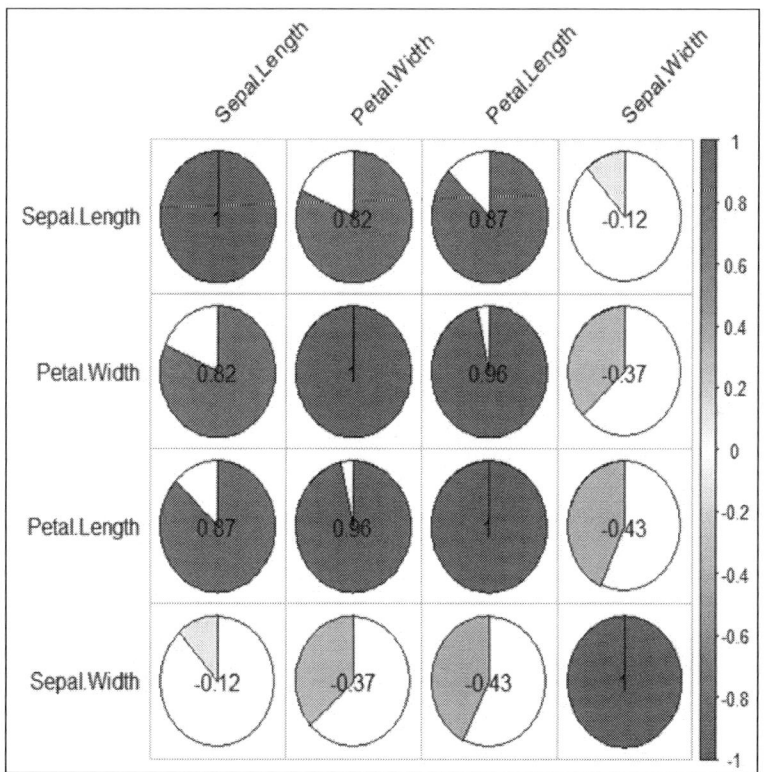

Exploration by end-user interfaces

So far we have seen and implemented some exploration tools from the R console. As an additional value, we will show you, very briefly, the exploration of data by using a tool that brings together many features related to data mining from R, Togaware Rattle.

To enter Rattle, we need to have previously installed it. Subsequently you need to type the following commands from the console:

```
# Set language to English
Sys.setenv(LANGUAGE="en")
#Load Rattle Package
suppressWarnings(suppressMessages(library(rattle)))
# Load visual interface
rattle()
```

 For more details about Rattle, for example, aspects of installation or use, there is much information available online. Also, you can consult the book written by its creator, Graham J. Williams, *Data Mining with Rattle and R, Springer*.

Loading data into Rattle

Rattle does not demand interaction with the console. It's a good way to begin to use R or it can help us to make a quick analysis of regular sized datasets.

To load the Iris dataset from Rattle:

1. In the **Data** menu, using the file selector, we look for the `iris.csv` file.
2. We assign the field separator and decimal separator so that it matches with the working dataset.
3. We press the **Execute** button in the results window, and, as a result, variables are loaded and the data type is displayed.
4. In order to visualize the data, we can use the **View** button.

This can be seen in the following screenshot:

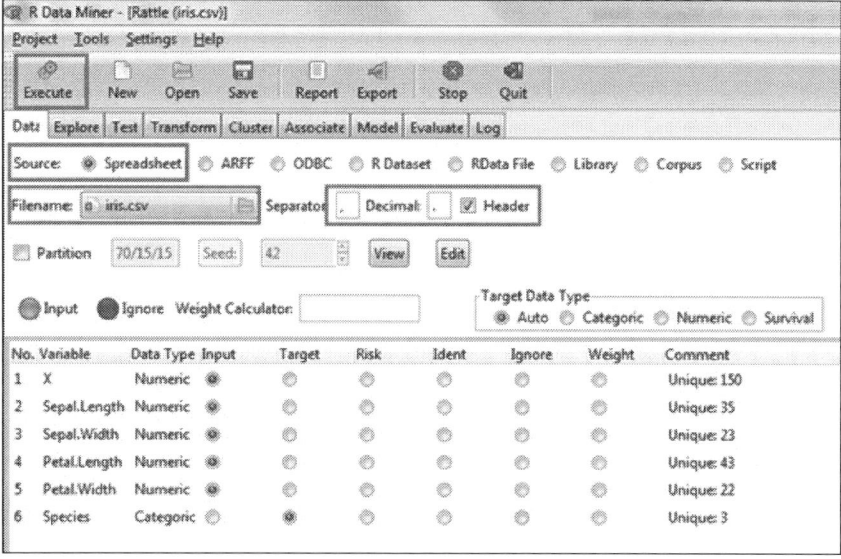

Basic exploration of dataset in Rattle

The basic exploration options are found in the **Explore | Summary** menu. We simply select the different options and press the **Execute** button. This can be seen in the following screenshot:

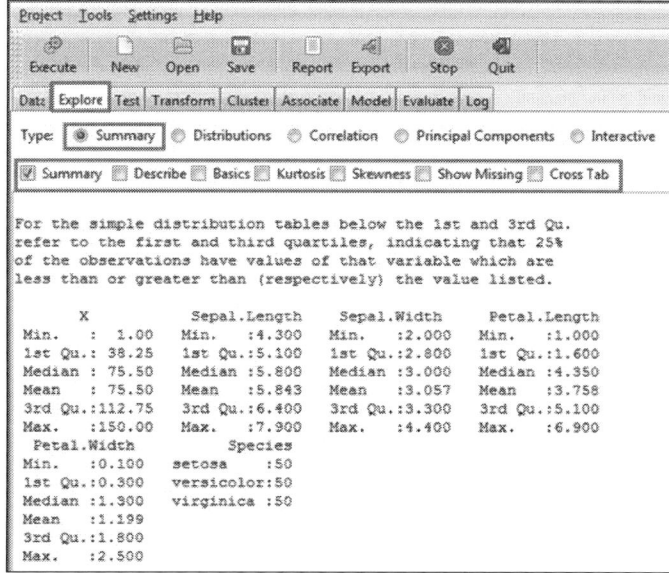

Exploring data by graphs in Rattle

The options for data exploration using graphs are found in the **Explore | Distributions** menu. We simply select the different options and press the **Execute** button. Rattle proceeds to generate histograms or boxplots displays. This can be seen in the following screenshot:

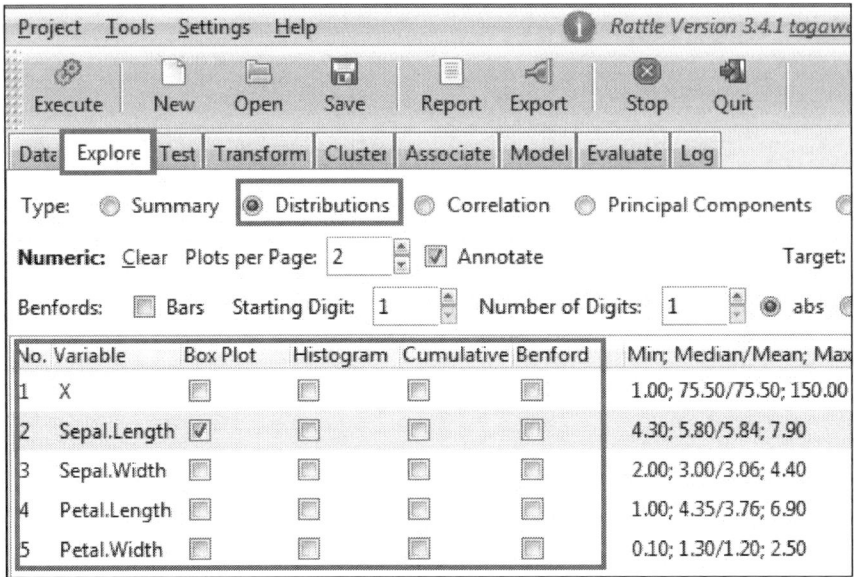

Exploring relations in data using Rattle

The options for correlation analysis are located in the **Explore | Correlations** menu. We simply select the different options and press the **Execute** button, and Rattle proceeds to generate summarizations and visualizations. This can be seen in the following screenshot:

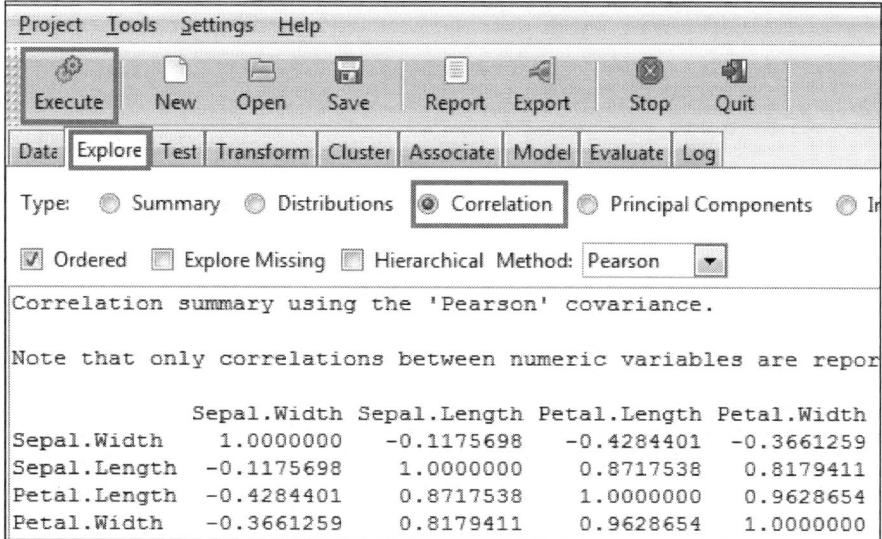

Summary

In this chapter, we discussed the importance of exploratory data analysis. We covered some of the basic data mining techniques. We began with loading data into the R environment and subsequently turned to the basics of summarization. From there, we moved to the construction of exploratory visualizations, ending with correlation analysis and graphic expression.

Additionally, we briefly mentioned a visual interface tool, as it can be used as a support for making a quick analysis without having to interact with the R console directly.

The content of this chapter is not intended to be exhaustive or exclusive. There are many approaches, tools, and techniques that can be used in the exploratory phase of analysis. However, we hope that it will help you to create a style or at least know about the different tools available.

In the next chapter, we will learn about one of the most used techniques in unsupervised learning—the clustering analysis. Identifying groups can discover and help to explain some patterns hiding in data; and it is frequently the solution for many problems.

3
Identifying and Understanding Groups – Clustering Algorithms

This chapter aims to explain one of the most used techniques in unsupervised learning, the **Clustering Analysis**. Identifying groups can uncover and help to explain some patterns hiding in data and it is frequently the answer for multiple problems in many industries or contexts. Finding clusters can help to uncover relationships in data, which can, in turn, be used to support future decisions.

It is considered an unsupervised learning technique since its objective is to find relationships between study variables, but not the relations that these variables may have in relation to a target variable.

Typically, the application of clustering techniques involves five phases: developing a working dataset, preprocessing and standardization of data, finding clusters in the data, interpreting those clusters, and finding conclusions.

In terms of this book, we have to start at stage two, since these kinds of techniques are heavily influenced by the state of the data, and so it is important to give them some treatment in most cases, for example, rescaling variables, or dealing with missing values, which are aspects that greatly affect the outcome.

As we have seen in previous chapters, R is a programming language that is very versatile with regard to data management and has a wide range of packages for modeling. In this chapter, we will discuss some of their potential in relation to cluster analysis.

We will cover the following topics:

- Transforming data
- K-Means clustering
- Hierarchical clustering
- Clustering by end-user tools

Transforming data

Actually, it is normal for us to spend a lot of time dealing with data. In fact, when data is good, the construction of models that will respond to our problems becomes easier.

Indeed, while all models have adjustable parameters to improve performance, we must always consider that an improvement in the data usually has a positive impact on desired outcomes.

Considering that clustering models work with distances, they are especially influenced by the data that we use. Therefore, we have included this section of the book, although the aspects discussed below can be applied to many different models.

Moreover, it makes sense to take a look at this topic after the exploration techniques that we saw in *Chapter 2, Working with Data: Exploratory Data Analysis*, and, as usual, in the exploratory phase, the need for transformation is detected.

Rescaling data

Whichever model we use will assume different things about the data. In the case of clustering models, it is very important that data, from the different numerical variables, expressed on a similar scale. When distances are calculated, if the units are very different, we cannot get proper results. For example, if we are doing an analysis related to a group of people and we have, among other data, the dollar income and age of the subjects, a variable such as income could overshadow the age variable. For analysis, 20 years of age may be more important than a $10,000 income. However, when compared both by measure of distances, a clustering model might underestimate the importance of age.

In order to mitigate the problem of the scale of the data, we can use methods of standardization. The standardization is the process of adjusting the data to a specific range, for example, between 0 and 1 or between –1 and 1. The following graph visually explains what would happen in a transformation between 0 and 1:

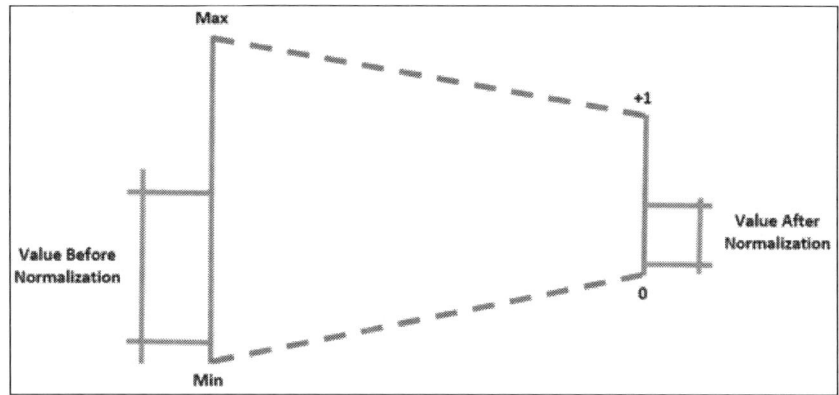

Looking at the previous figure, the value before being transformed is located between a minimum and a maximum value. A normalization process *between 0-1* takes place and these become the new limits: a minimum value of 0 and a maximum value of 1. The new data is not specified in the original unit of measurement but still maintains relationships and proportionality between them.

There are several techniques for normalization; we will see some in the following sections.

Recenter

The recenter performs a standard z-score transformation. The variable's mean value is subtracted from each value and each one is then divided by the standard deviation. The resulting variable will have a mean of 0 and a standard deviation of 1:

Recenter – Z score

$$Z = \frac{X - \mu}{\sigma}$$

Let's see how we can make a normalization of this kind in R. For this, we will work with a new dataset, which is located in the following package of CRAN:

- **Package**: ElemStatLearn
- **Dataset**: Prostate
- **Description**:

  前列腺特异性抗原、

  Data to examine the correlation between the level of prostate-specific antigens and the number of clinical measures in men who are about to receive a radical prostatectomy. —→ 前列腺切除术

- **Features**: lcavol log cancer volume, lweight log prostate weight, age in years, lbph log of the amount of benign prostatic hyperplasia, svi seminal vesicle invasion, lcp log of capsular penetration, gleason a numeric vector, pgg45 percent of Gleason score 4 or 5, lpsa response

```
# Load dataset from csv file
#data <- read.table("prostate.csv", header = TRUE,
#sep = ",", #dec = ".",row.names=1)
# Load dataset from package in CRAN
 suppressWarnings(
        suppressMessages(if
                        (!require(ElemStatLearn))
                install.packages("ElemStatLearn")))
 library("ElemStatLearn")


# Create a data.frame named data

data(prostate)
data<-prostate[1:9]
```

> For convenience, in the following examples, we will be working only with the first four variables of the dataset, by indexing instructions like the following:
>
> data [1: 4]

Once the data is loaded, we can use the library scale to implement a normalization of them, Scale: Scaling and Centering of Matrix-like Objects:

```
# Show the head of dataset Before Recenter

head(data[1:4])


      lcavol  lweight age       lbph
1 -0.5798185 2.769459  50 -1.386294
2 -0.9942523 3.319626  58 -1.386294
3 -0.5108256 2.691243  74 -1.386294
4 -1.2039728 3.282789  58 -1.386294
5  0.7514161 3.432373  62 -1.386294
6 -1.0498221 3.228826  50 -1.386294
```

The previous code shows the original dataset for the four selected variables. As shown, the differences of scale are important, especially in the case of the variable age:

```
# Using the scale function to recenter data

recenter<-as.data.frame(scale(data[1:4]))
# Show the head of dataset After Recenter

head(recenter)

      lcavol    lweight       age       lbph
1 -1.6373556 -2.0062118 -1.8624260 -1.024706
2 -1.9889805 -0.7220088 -0.7878962 -1.024706
3 -1.5788189 -2.1887840  1.3611634 -1.024706
4 -2.1669171 -0.8079939 -0.7878962 -1.024706
5 -0.5078745 -0.4588340 -0.2506313 -1.024706
6 -2.0361285 -0.9339546 -1.8624260 -1.024706
```

After transformation, the variables are not expressed in their original scales, for example, age no longer displays a number of years.

To make it interesting while performing a test, we can confirm that the transformation does not affect the relationship between the variables:

```
# comparing correlations

# Data before transformation
cor(data[1:4])
            lcavol    lweight       age       lbph
lcavol   1.0000000 0.2805214 0.2249999 0.0273497
lweight  0.2805214 1.0000000 0.3479691 0.4422644
age      0.2249999 0.3479691 1.0000000 0.3501859
lbph     0.0273497 0.4422644 0.3501859 1.0000000

# Data after transformation
cor(recenter)
            lcavol    lweight       age       lbph
lcavol   1.0000000 0.2805214 0.2249999 0.0273497
lweight  0.2805214 1.0000000 0.3479691 0.4422644
age      0.2249999 0.3479691 1.0000000 0.3501859
lbph     0.0273497 0.4422644 0.3501859 1.0000000
```

It may be considered a good practice to keep the original values (before transforming) within the dataset. This can be done in many ways, and one way is as follows:

```
# Transform variables by rescaling.
# Rescale lcavol
data[["RRC_lcavol"]] <- data[["lcavol"]]

# Recenter and rescale data
      data[["RRC_lcavol"]] <-
            scale(data[["lcavol"]])[,1]

# Rescale lweight
      data[["RRC_lweight"]] <- data[["lweight"]]

# Recenter and rescale data
      data[["RRC_lweight"]] <-
            scale(data[["lweight"]])[,1]

# Show the original and recenter together
head(data[c('lcavol','RRC_lcavol','lweight',
         'RRC_lweight')])

      lcavol RRC_lcavol  lweight RRC_lweight
1 -0.5798185 -1.6373556 2.769459  -2.0062118
2 -0.9942523 -1.9889805 3.319626  -0.7220088
3 -0.5108256 -1.5788189 2.691243  -2.1887840
4 -1.2039728 -2.1669171 3.282789  -0.8079939
5  0.7514161 -0.5078745 3.432373  -0.4588340
6 -1.0498221 -2.0361285 3.228826  -0.9339546
```

Scale [0-1]

Another method for make transformation is the Scale [0-1]: just rescale the original values into the 0-1 range. This is done by subtracting the minimum value from the variable's value for each observation and, then, dividing by the difference between the minimum and the maximum values:

Scale [0-1]

$$Z_i = \frac{X_i - min(x)}{max(x) - min(x)}$$

If we want to implement this transformation method, we can use the reshape package, in particular the rescaler function:

```
# Transform variables by rescaling.

#Loading or installing package reshape
suppressWarnings(
        suppressMessages(if
                         (!require(reshape, quietly=TRUE))
                install.packages("reshape")))
library("reshape")

# Rescaling data to Scale [0-1] using reshape

dataR01<-rescaler(data, "range")
# Comparing original vs scaled

tail(data[1:4])

     lcavol  lweight age      lbph
92 2.532903 3.677566  61  1.3480732
93 2.830268 3.876396  68 -1.3862944
94 3.821004 3.896909  44 -1.3862944
95 2.907447 3.396185  52 -1.3862944
96 2.882564 3.773910  68  1.5581446
97 3.471966 3.974998  68  0.4382549

tail(dataR01[1:4])

     lcavol   lweight        age      lbph
92 0.7507582 0.5415392 0.52631579 0.7365109
93 0.8082970 0.6241964 0.71052632 0.0000000
94 1.0000000 0.6327240 0.07894737 0.0000000
95 0.8232309 0.4245640 0.28947368 0.0000000
96 0.8184160 0.5815911 0.71052632 0.7930944
97 0.9324629 0.6651870 0.71052632 0.4914484
```

Again, the variables change the scales at which they are expressed. However, as has been seen, this does not change the relationship between the variables.

Median/MAD

Median/MAD is a robust version of the standard recenter transform.

The median value is subtracted from each value, and each is then divided by the median absolute deviation. The resulting variable will have a median of 0.

It is better for outliers than the normal z-score:

Median / MAD

$$Z = \frac{X - Me}{MAD}$$

The function is included in the `reshape` package and its use is very similar to the previous example:

```
# Transform variables by rescaling.
#Loading or installing package reshape
suppressWarnings(
        suppressMessages(if
                        (!require(reshape, quietly=TRUE))
                install.packages("reshape")))
library("reshape")
# Rescaling data to Scale [0-1] using reshape

dataMAD<-rescaler(data, "robust")

# Comparing original vs scaled

head(data[1:4])
      lcavol  lweight age      lbph
1 -0.5798185 2.769459  50 -1.386294
2 -0.9942523 3.319626  58 -1.386294
3 -0.5108256 2.691243  74 -1.386294
4 -1.2039728 3.282789  58 -1.386294
5  0.7514161 3.432373  62 -1.386294
6 -1.0498221 3.228826  50 -1.386294

head(dataMAD[1:4])
      lcavol    lweight        age       lbph
```

```
1 -1.5809071 -2.2720412 -2.5293403 -0.6744908
2 -1.9041761 -0.8075634 -1.1803588 -0.6744908
3 -1.5270909 -2.4802427  1.5176042 -0.6744908
4 -2.0677635 -0.9056190 -1.1803588 -0.6744908
5 -0.5425101 -0.5074446 -0.5058681 -0.6744908
6 -1.9475220 -1.0492620 -2.5293403 -0.6744908
```

Natural log

不对称

Transformation using logarithms is useful when the dataset contains variables whose distribution has a high skewness level (asymmetry). A good example is the income of a group of people: If we imagine a histogram of income, considering that most people earn less money and a few earn much more, that distribution would have a substantial skewness, caused by these outliers.

It is important to consider that this type of transformation can cause *infinite* values that should be posteriorly recoded.

Let's see how this transformation can be applied in R:

```
# LogN transformation for Age
dataLogN <- log(data$age)
# Replace Inf's
dataLogN[dataLogN == -Inf] <- NA
# Comparing original vs scaled

head(data$age)

[1]  50 58 74 58 62 50

head(dataLogN)

[1]  3.912023 4.060443 4.304065 4.060443 4.127134 3.912023
```

数据重建

Imputation of missing data

The data imputation is the process through which we proceed to replace missing values in the dataset for other values that make sense. However, it is very important to understand that there are not always valid treatments for missing values. Missing values exist for many reasons; understanding these reasons and having knowledge of the data is what allows providing appropriate treatment.

Zero/Missing

This uses a constant value to replace each missing value in the selected variable(s).

For example, this can be a good choice if missing values are likely to indicate a 0.

```
# we will create a new variable for imputation

data[["Sons"]] <- round(data$age/10,0)-3
data$Sons[data$Sons==4]<-NA

# Finding the missing data in dataset

NewData<-(data[c('age','Sons','lcavol','lweight')])
head(NewData[!complete.cases(NewData),],10)

    age Sons     lcavol  lweight
3    74   NA -0.5108256 2.691243
14   67   NA  1.4770487 2.998229
16   66   NA  1.5411591 3.061052
17   70   NA -0.4155154 3.516013
18   66   NA  2.2884862 3.649359
20   70   NA  0.1823216 3.825375
25   69   NA  0.3852624 3.667400
26   68   NA  1.4469190 3.124565
28   67   NA -0.4004776 3.865979
29   67   NA  1.0402767 3.128951

# Zero/Missing Imputation
data$Sons[is.na(data$Sons)] <- 0

# checking missing values
head(data[!complete.cases(data),])

[1] lcavol  lweight age     lbph    svi     lcp     gleason
<0 rows> (or 0-length row.names)
```

This kind of imputation works well in a case in which, for example, after conducting an investigation, we determined that the missing values in the number of children actually indicated that these people had no children, in which case, to replace missing values by zero is correct.

Mean imputation

The mean imputation uses the mean of the variable to replace each missing value.

An important aspect to consider is that this kind of imputation is not always recommended as it could change the variables distribution and, hence, result in poor models.

 Instead of using the media, it is also possible to use the median or the mode. However, this should be used very carefully since this kind of transformation changes the distribution of variables.

The following is an example of how the imputation of the mean values is performed to replace missing values:

```
# we will create some missing values in Age
data(prostate)
data<-prostate[1:9]
data$age[data$age==68]<-NA

#searching the missing data in dataset
NewData<-(data[c('age','lcavol','lweight')])

head(NewData[!complete.cases(NewData),],10)
   age   lcavol   lweight
26  NA  1.446919 3.124565
39  NA  2.660959 4.085136
42  NA  1.442202 3.682610
48  NA  1.163151 4.035125
51  NA  1.091923 3.993603
54  NA  2.127041 4.121473
67  NA  2.022871 3.878466
76  NA  3.141130 3.263849
91  NA  3.246491 4.101817
93  NA  2.830268 3.876396

# Mean Imputation in Age
 data$age[is.na(data$age)] <- round(mean(data$age, na.rm=TRUE),0)
 head(data[!complete.cases(data),],10)

[1] lcavol  lweight age     lbph    svi     lcp     gleason
<0 rows> (or 0-length row.names)
```

Finally, as an alternative to the imputation of missing data, if we have enough data, we can decide to delete the data with missing values. It's a valid approach and possibly the most frequently used.

✴ Fundamentals of clustering techniques

Clustering is based on the concepts of similarity and distance, while proximity is determined by a distance function. It allows the generation of clusters where each of these groups consists of individuals who have common features with each other.

Overall, the analysis of clusters is similar to the classification models, with the difference that the groups are not preset. The goal is to perform a partition of data into clusters that can be disjoint or not.

An important point in clustering techniques is that the groups are not given a priori and this implies that the person doing the analysis should support the interpretation of the groups found.

There are many methods, and the most popular are based on Hierarchical Classification and dynamic clouds or K-Means.

The K-Means clustering

In very general terms, the K-Means algorithm aims to partition a set of observations into clusters so that each observation belongs to the cluster that possesses the nearest mean.

Although it is a computationally difficult problem, there are very efficient implementations to quickly find the local optimum. In an optimization problem, the optimum is the value that maximizes or minimizes the condition that we are looking for.

Given a set of observations *(X1, X2, …, XN)*, K-Means clustering aims to partition the N observations into $K (\leq N)$ sets S = *{S1, S2, …, Sk}* so as to minimize the **within-cluster sum of squares (WCSS)**:

K-Means objective is to find:

$$\underset{S}{arg\,min} \sum_{i=1}^{k} \sum_{x \in S_i} \| x - \mu_i \|^2$$

Where μ_i is the mean of points in S_i.

The intention of this book is not to enter in deep mathematical detail; however, it is important to understand the standard algorithm, assuming that we are seeking to create three clusters, that is, $k = 3$:

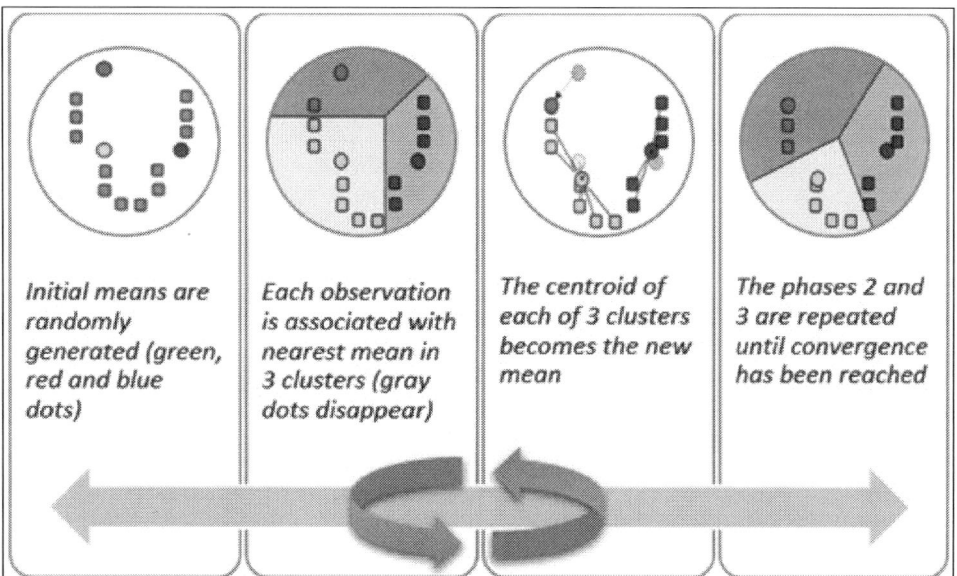

| Initial means are randomly generated (green, red and blue dots) | Each observation is associated with nearest mean in 3 clusters (gray dots disappear) | The centroid of each of 3 clusters becomes the new mean | The phases 2 and 3 are repeated until convergence has been reached |

The method of Forgy and Random partition are the most common initialization approaches. Forgy chooses k observations from the data and uses these as the initial means. The method first assigns a cluster to each observation at random, then proceeds to the update phase, thereby computing the initial mean to become the centroid of the cluster's randomly assigned points. The assignment phase is also referred to as the expectation phase, and the update phase as the maximization phase, making this algorithm a variant of the generalized expectation maximization algorithm.

In R, there are several packages that allow us to use K-Means. The following is an implementation using the Iris dataset, which we already worked in the previous chapter:

```
# K Means
# Load the Iris dataset (see chapter 2 for details)
  Iris<-iris

# Show the head of numerical section of dataset
head(Iris[1:4])

  Sepal.Length Sepal.Width Petal.Length Petal.Width
1          5.1         3.5          1.4         0.2
```

2	4.9	3.0	1.4	0.2
3	4.7	3.2	1.3	0.2
4	4.6	3.1	1.5	0.2
5	5.0	3.6	1.4	0.2
6	5.4	3.9	1.7	0.4

```
# Build the K-Means standard model
set.seed(42)
KM.Iris<-kmeans(Iris[1:4], 3,iter.max=1000,
algorithm = c("Forgy") )
```

At this point, we have created a model for K-Means clustering and that is stored in the *KM.Iris* object. We can see some information about the outcome:

```
# Get some information about the model built
# Size of clusters

KM.Iris$size

[1] 62 38 50

# Centers of clusters three clusters by variable
KM.Iris$centers

  Sepal.Length Sepal.Width Petal.Length Petal.Width
1     5.901613    2.748387     4.393548    1.433871
2     6.850000    3.073684     5.742105    2.071053
3     5.006000    3.428000     1.462000    0.246000

# Table with Clusters recounts by species
  table(Iris$Species,KM.Iris$cluster)

             1  2  3
  setosa     0  0 50
  versicolor 48  2  0
  virginica  14 36  0
```

We must remember that clustering is not a method for classification. In fact, we should not know the species mapped in the Iris dataset. For teaching purposes, they are compared here to see how the clustering model works.

Based on the numerical data of Iris, model K-Means builds three groups, as we indicated, and then proceeds to classify each observation, in one of those groups. All of the type Setosa were assigned to group 3, most of the plants in group 2 are type Virginica, and group 1 has had assigned all plants type Versicolor and part of plants type Virginica.

It is interesting to plot the result. This allows for a better appreciation of the information, so we must reduce the dataset to be represented in two dimensions:

```
# Translate into a two dimensions using
# Multidimensional scaling.
Iris.dist <- dist(Iris[1:4])
Iris.mds <- cmdscale(Iris.dist)
# Plot points in 2 dimensional space
# Open a multiple plots array
par(mfrow = c(1, 2))
# Load or install the package scatterplot3d
suppressWarnings(
        suppressMessages(if
                        (!require(scatterplot3d, quietly=TRUE))
                install.packages("scatterplot3d")))
library("scatterplot3d ")
# Set the characters points to 1,2,3 numbers
chars <- c("1", "2", "3")[as.integer(iris$Species)]
# Plot a 3d Graphic
g3d=scatterplot3d(Iris.mds,pch=chars)
g3d$points3d(Iris.mds,col=KM.Iris$cluster,pch=chars)
# Plot a 2d Graphic
plot(Iris.mds, col = KM.Iris$cluster, pch = chars, xlab =
"Index", ylab = "Y")
```

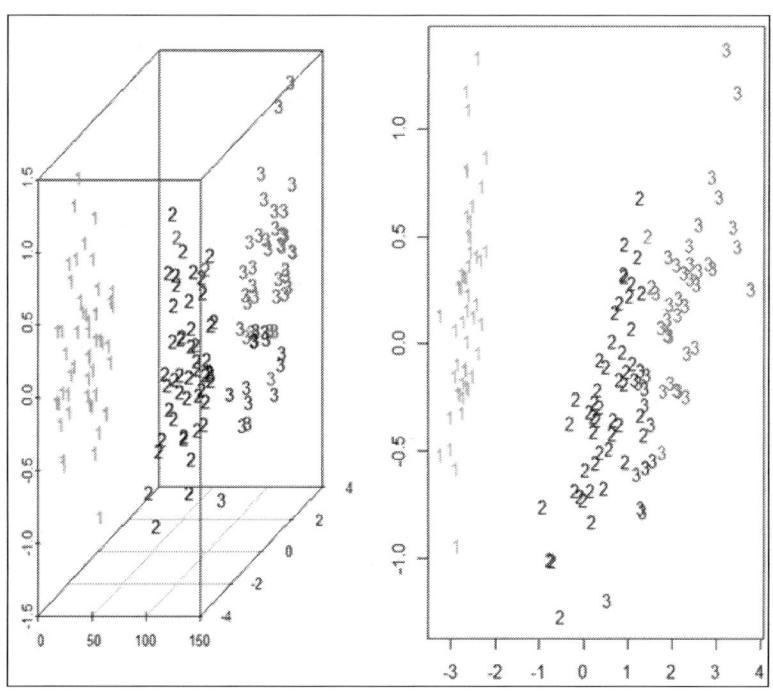

The graphic expression of clusters can help to evaluate whether the result makes sense. If we determine that it does, we can also include the results of cluster analysis in the original dataset. Then we can work on R or also export it to other tools:

```
# Add cluster to original dataset
Iris.Cluster<-cbind(Iris,KM.Iris[1])

head(Iris.Cluster[3:6])

   Petal.Length Petal.Width Species cluster
1           1.4         0.2  setosa       3
2           1.4         0.2  setosa       3
3           1.3         0.2  setosa       3
4           1.5         0.2  setosa       3
5           1.4         0.2  setosa       3
6           1.7         0.4  setosa       3
```

The K-Means function requires that we properly define two important parameters: the number of clusters that it is convenient to use and the type of the function algorithm to be used to establish the optimum.

Defining the number of clusters

One of the most frequent questions in relation to the use of K-Means is the definition of the number of clusters to be used. Considering the impact that this can have on the outcome of the analysis we do, we will dedicate part of this chapter to make some recommendations about how to set this parameter.

Remember that the goal of the clustering algorithm is to minimize the within-cluster sum of squares.

We can make a first approximation using current computational capacity. You can create a repeating cycle or loop that generates a large amount of K-Means models, in which, on each iteration, the value of K is increased by 1.

The location of the elbow in the resulting plot suggests a suitable number of clusters for the K-Means:

```
# 30 K Means Loop
InerIC = rep(0, 30)
for (k in 1:30) {
    set.seed(42)
    groups = kmeans(Iris[1:4], k)
    InerIC[k] = groups$tot.withinss
}
```

```
plot(InerIC, col = "blue", type = "b")
abline(v = 4, col = "black", lty = 3)
text(4, 60, "4 Clusters", col = "black", adj = c(0,
    -0.1), cex = 0.7)
```

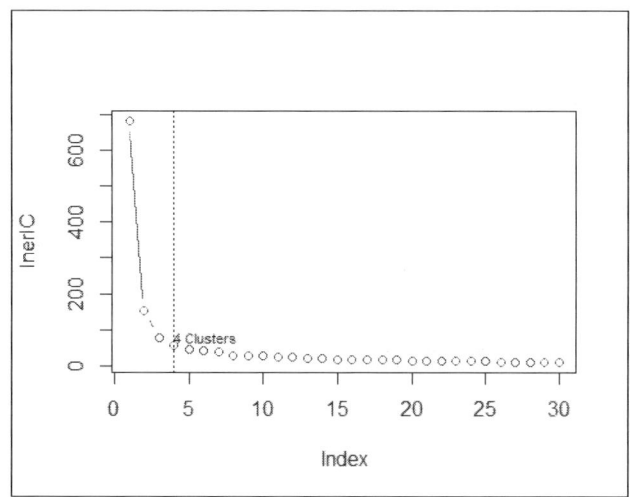

The preceding graph works for a visual approach. At this point, we can approximate the amount of appropriate clusters, and there would be between three and four clusters, which, at first, seems to make sense, given what we know of the Iris dataset.

We can use many other methods individually; however, I recommend the use of a package that integrates 30 methods to determine the optimal number of clusters, the NbClust package:

The NbClust package provides 30 indices for determining the number of clusters and proposes to the user the best clustering scheme from the different results obtained by varying all combinations of number of clusters, distance measures, and clustering methods.

The package decided by *voting* considers all indices on a count, as the number of clusters that each method chosen as the best option, so that the number of clusters having more frequently, that is, who receives more votes, it is considered the best option.

It's a great way to compare indices, and if we do not want to use the package's recommendation, we can reach our own conclusions when using the information that it generates.

In the following we find the suggested amount of clusters, directly in R, using the NbClust package:

```
# Load or install the NbClust Package
suppressWarnings(suppressMessages(if (!require(NbClust,
    quietly = TRUE)) install.packages("NbClust")))
library("NbClust")
# Load the dataset Iris and assign the numerical
# variables to a new data frame 'data'.

Iris <- iris
data <- Iris[, -5]

# Find the best number of clusters using all
# indices
Best <- NbClust(data, diss = NULL, distance = "euclidean",
    min.nc = 2, max.nc = 15, method = "complete", index =
"alllong")
```

By default, once finalized, the NbClust package offers a summary of the main results of the vote of the 30 indices:

```
*******************************************************************
* Among all indices:
* 2 proposed 2 as the best number of clusters
* 15 proposed 3 as the best number of clusters
* 5 proposed 4 as the best number of clusters
* 1 proposed 6 as the best number of clusters
* 1 proposed 14 as the best number of clusters
* 3 proposed 15 as the best number of clusters

                ***** Conclusion *****
 * According to the majority rule, the best number of
clusters is  3


*******************************************************************
```

An important thing to note in the preceding example is that we use a wide range of clusters when we use the NbClust function: min.nc = 2, max.nc = 15. This causes a more distributed voting. However, in this case, 55 percent of indices vote for three clusters, which we know is right for the Iris dataset.

The package also has some graphical indices.

The Hubert index is a graphical method for determining the number of clusters, and in a Hubert index plot, we seek a knee that corresponds to a significant increase of the value of the measure:

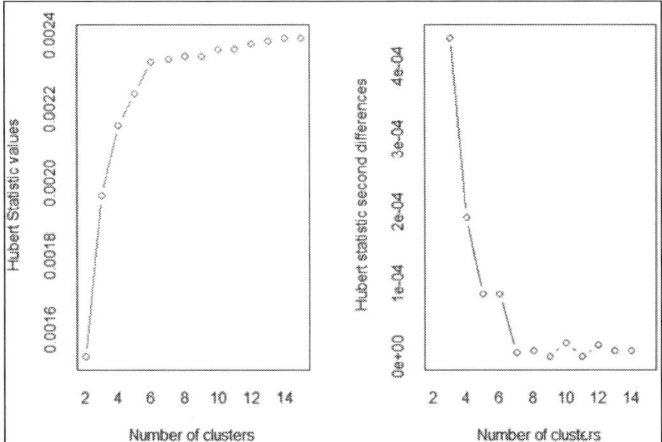

The D index is a graphical method for determining the number of clusters. In the D index plot, we seek a significant knee that corresponds to a significant increase of the value of the measure:

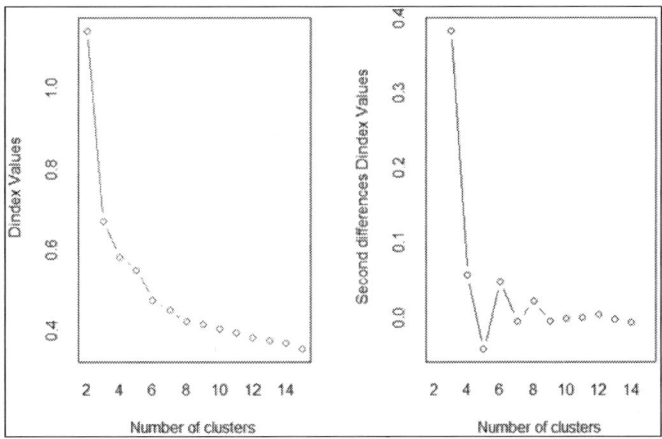

In addition to the default information, `NbClust` stores valuable information in the object being created. In our example, we call that object as `Best`. For example, if we want to see the exact count of the vote for each index, we could create a table whose rows show the choice of each index in relation to the number of clusters:

```
#Build a table with results of indices
```

```
table(names(Best$Best.nc[1,]),
      Best$Best.nc[1,])
```

```
           0 1 2 3 4 6 14 15
Ball       0 0 0 1 0 0  0  0
Beale      0 0 0 1 0 0  0  0
CCC        0 0 0 1 0 0  0  0
CH         0 0 0 0 1 0  0  0
Cindex     0 0 0 1 0 0  0  0
DB         0 0 0 1 0 0  0  0
Dindex     1 0 0 0 0 0  0  0
Duda       0 0 0 0 1 0  0  0
Dunn       0 0 0 0 0 0  0  1
Frey       0 1 0 0 0 0  0  0
Friedman   0 0 0 0 1 0  0  0
Gamma      0 0 0 0 0 0  1  0
Gap        0 0 0 1 0 0  0  0
Gplus      0 0 0 0 0 0  0  1
Hartigan   0 0 0 1 0 0  0  0
```

If you do not want to make a table and prefer visual support, we could make a frequency graph with the count:

```
# sets 1x2 grid for Plotting
par(mfrow = c(1, 2))

# Making Graph of recounts
hist(Best$Best.nc[1,],
     breaks = max(na.omit(Best$Best.nc[1,])))

barplot(table(Best$Best.nc[1,]))
```

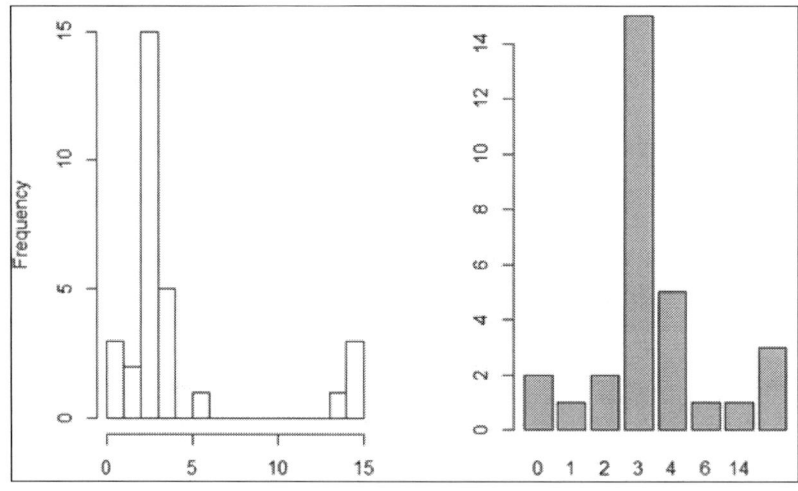

Looking at the preceding chart, we can quickly see that most of the indices proposed three clusters as the best alternative for the Iris dataset.

Defining the cluster K-Mean algorithm

Clustering models generated by K-Means can use several different algorithms and that affects the overall outcome of the analysis. Considering that not all datasets are equal, it is important to test the algorithms to determine which one fits best.

We won't explain each algorithm in depth, but we will explain how we can choose between them, in a practical way:

```
## Choosing between 4 algorithms

# Set vectors for storing results
Hartigan <- 0
Lloyd <- 0
Forgy <- 0
MacQueen <- 0
# to make it reproducible
set.seed(42)
# Running 500 KMeans with 3 clusters and 1000 max
# iterations for each method
for (i in 1:500) {
    KM <- kmeans(Iris[1:4], 3, iter.max = 1000, algorithm =
"Hartigan-Wong")
    Hartigan <- Hartigan + KM$betweenss
    KM <- kmeans(Iris[1:4], 3, iter.max = 1000, algorithm =
"Lloyd")
    Lloyd <- Lloyd + KM$betweenss
    KM <- kmeans(Iris[1:4], 3, iter.max = 1000, algorithm =
"Forgy")
    Forgy <- Forgy + KM$betweenss
    KM <- kmeans(Iris[1:4], 3, iter.max = 1000, algorithm =
"MacQueen")
    MacQueen <- MacQueen + KM$betweenss
}
# Build a data frame with results
Methods <- c("Hartigan-Wong", "Lloyd", "Forgy", "MacQueen")
Results <- as.data.frame(round(c(Hartigan, Lloyd, Forgy,
    MacQueen)/500, 2))
Results <- cbind(Methods, Results)
names(Results) <- c("Method", "Betweenss")

Results
```

The data frame `Results` stores the averages `betweenss`, calculated as a result of 500 iterations. Considering that the intention is to maximize the `betweenss`, then, the best algorithm could be Hartingan - Wong:

```
    Results
            Method Betweenss
1 Hartigan-Wong    591.14
2          Lloyd   588.47
3          Forgy   589.62
4        MacQueen  589.67
```

Alternatives for plotting clusters

In addition to traditional charts, we can use special alternatives for cluster analysis. These variants will help in the analysis of groups and also in the presentation of results:

```
par(mfrow = c(1, 1))
# Load Iris Data
Iris<-iris
# K-Means Clustering with 3 clusters

KM <-kmeans(Iris[1:4], 3, iter.max = 1000, algorithm = "Hartigan-
Wong")

# Load or install the library Cluster
suppressWarnings(
        suppressMessages(if
                            (!require(cluster, quietly=TRUE))
                    install.packages("cluster")))
    library("cluster")

# Cluster Plot against 1st 2 principal components
clusplot(Iris[1:4], KM$cluster, color=TRUE, shade=TRUE,
        labels=2, lines=1,main='Cluster Analysis for Iris')
```

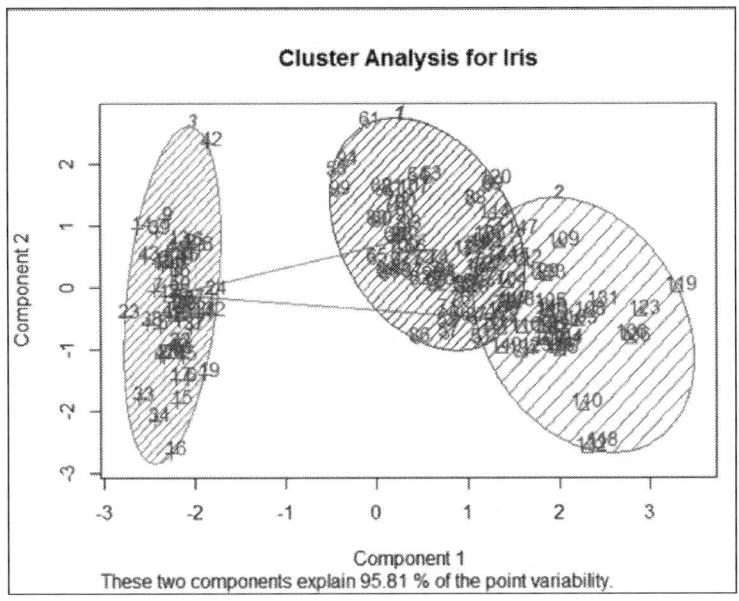

Another interesting alternative is to use "Silhouettes" graphics through which each cluster is represented, based on the comparison of "tightness" and "separation":

```
# Load or Install packages
suppressWarnings(suppressMessages(if (!require(HSAUR,
    quietly = TRUE)) install.packages("HSAUR")))
suppressWarnings(suppressMessages(if (!require(cluster,
    quietly = TRUE)) install.packages("cluster")))
library("HSAUR")
library("cluster")


# K-Means Clustering with 3 clusters
KM <- kmeans(Iris[1:4], 3, iter.max = 1000, algorithm = "Hartigan-
Wong")

# Dissimilarity Matrix Calculation
diss <- daisy(Iris[1:4])
dE2 <- diss^2

# silhouette Calculation
obj <- silhouette(KM$cl, dE2)
```

```
# Making a silhouette Plot
plot(obj, col = c("red", "green", "blue"))
```

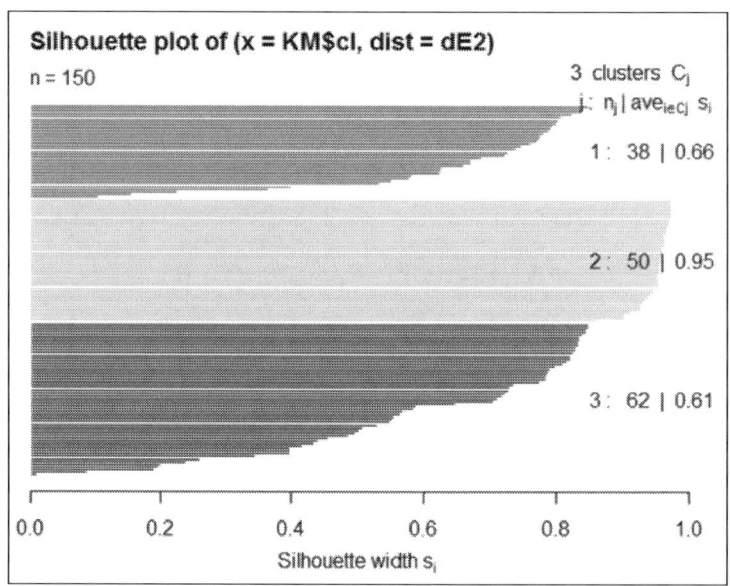

If you want to delve into the construction and interpretation of silhouette graphics, refer to the article at http://www.sciencedirect.com/science/article/pii/0377042787901257.

Hierarchical clustering

Another one of the most used methods for clustering analysis is the **Hierarchical Clustering Analysis (HCA)**. This method, as its name suggests, aims to build a hierarchy of clusters and generally this is done in two ways:

- **Agglomerative methods**: This method uses a bottom up approach in which each observation begins in its own clusters and pairs of cluster are merged as one moves up the Hierarchical structure.

- **Divisive methods**: This method uses a top-down approach in which each of the observations begin in one cluster and split recursively as one moves up the Hierarchical structure.

The agglomerative methods, using a recursive algorithm that follows the next phases:

- Find the two closest points in the dataset
- Link these points and consider them as a single point
- The process starts again, now using the new dataset that contains the new point

This methodology requires measuring the distance between points. The aim is that the measured distances between observations of the same cluster are as small as possible and the distances between clusters are as large as possible.

In a hierarchical clustering, there are two very important parameters in relation to the above: the **distance metric** and the **linkage method**.

Clustering distance metric

Defining closeness is a fundamental aspect. If you don't use a metric for distance that makes sense with your dataset, it is quite possible that you won't get any useful information from your cluster analyses.

A measure of dissimilarity is that which defines clusters that will be combined in the case of agglomerative method, or that, in the case of divisive clustering method, when these are to be divided.

The main measures of distance are as follows:

Distance Metric	Definition
Euclidean Distance	Usual square distance between the two vectors (2 norm)
Maximum Distance	Maximum distance between two components of x and y (supremum norm)
Manhattan Distance	Absolute distance between the two vectors (1 norm)
Canberra Distance	It is a weighted version of L1 (Manhattan) distance. sum($|x\_i - y\_i|$ / $|x\_i + y\_i|$). Terms with zero numerator and denominator are omitted from the sum and treated as if the values were missing
Binary Distance	The vectors are regarded as binary bits, so non-zero elements are *on* and zero elements are *off*. The distance is the proportion of bits in which only one is *on* among those in which at least one is *on*

Distance Metric	Definition
Pearson Distance	Also named *not centered Pearson* *sum(x_i y_i) / sqrt [sum(x_i^2) sum(y_i^2)]*
Correlation	Also named *Centered Pearson 1 - corr(x,y)*
Spearman Distance	Compute a distance based on rank. sum *(d_i^2)* where *d_i* is the difference in rank between *x_i* and *y_i*

Linkage methods

The linkage methods determine how the distance between two clusters is defined. A linkage rule is necessary for calculating the inter-cluster distances.

It is important to try several linkage methods to compare their results. Depending on the dataset, some methods may work better. The following is a list of the most common linkage methods:

Linkage Methods	Definition
Single Linkage	The distance between two clusters is the minimum distance between an observation in one cluster and an observation in the other cluster. A good choice when clusters are obviously separated.
Complete Linkage	The distance between two clusters is the maximum distance between an observation in one cluster and an observation in the other cluster. It can be sensitive to outliers.
Average Linkage	The distance between two clusters is the mean distance between an observation in one cluster and an observation in the other cluster.
Centroid Linkage	The distance between two clusters is the distance between the cluster centroids or means.
Median Linkage	The distance between two clusters is the median distance between an observation in one cluster and an observation in the other cluster. It reduces the effect of outliers.
Ward Linkage	The distance between two clusters is the sum of the squared deviations from points to centroids. Try to minimize the within-cluster sum of squares. It can be sensitive to outliers.
McQuitty Linkage	When two clusters A and B are be joined, the distance to new cluster C is the average of distances of A and B to C. So, the distance depends on a combination of clusters instead of individual observations in the clusters.

Hierarchical clustering in R

There are many implementations of hierarchical clustering in R. The following is an example of how you could build a model directly from the console.

For the following example, we will use a dataset of UC Irvine Machine Learning Repository, the Zoo Dataset. It contains 100 animals and 17 features for each one.

The aim of the example is to build a model based on hierarchical clustering, in which animals are classified by their characteristics.

 The UCI Machine Learning Repository is a collection of databases, domain theories, and data generators that are used by the machine learning community for the empirical analysis of machine learning algorithms. The archive was created as an ftp archive in 1987 by David Aha and fellow graduate students at UC Irvine; refer to `http://archive.ics.uci.edu/ml/index.html`.

The first thing to do is get the data, and since these are published on a website, we will take the opportunity to show how it is possible to make a direct extraction of data published on a web page:

```
# Reading Data from UCI Repository Online
animals <- read.table("https://archive.ics.uci.edu/ml/machine-
learning-databases/zoo/zoo.data",
    sep = ",", header = F, col.names = c("animal",
        "hair", "feathers", "eggs", "milk", "airbone",
        "aquatic", "predator", "toothed", "backbone",
        "breathes", "venomous", "fins", "legs", "tail",
        "domestic", "catsize", "type"), fill = FALSE,
    strip.white = T)


# Doing some data preparation

animals <- animals[, -18]
animals <- animals[-27, ]
animals <- animals[-29, ]
animal.names <- animals[, 1]
animals <- data.frame(row.names = animal.names, animals[2:17])


# Verifying the top of data loaded

head(animals[1:7], 5)
```

	hair	feathers	eggs	milk	airbone	aquatic	predator
aardvark	1	0	0	1	0	0	1
antelope	1	0	0	1	0	0	0
bass	0	0	1	0	0	1	1
bear	1	0	0	1	0	0	1
boar	1	0	0	1	0	0	1

In the preceding example, we loaded data directly from a web page. That's just an added value. It is also possible to load data from a comma separated file, as you know:

```
animals <- read.csv("file:///C:/Unsupervised Learning/Chapter
03/animals.csv",
    na.strings = c(".", "NA", "", "?"), strip.white = TRUE,
    encoding = "UTF-8")
```

Continuing the example, we can try to approximate an appropriate amount of clusters. However, this is only a reference, as the hierarchical clustering was not a prior classification of the number of groups.

To do this, you can use the NbClust package:

```
# Find the best number of clusters using all indices

suppressWarnings(suppressMessages(if (!require(NbClust,
    quietly = TRUE)) install.packages("NbClust")))
library("NbClust")

# Index only numerical data
data <- animals[1:16]

# define the indexes for work
ind <- c("kl", "ch", "hartigan", "cindex", "db", "silhouette",
    "duda", "pseudot2", "ratkowsky", "ball", "ptbiserial",
    "gap", "frey", "gamma", "gplus", "dunn", "sdindex",
    "sdbw")
clusters <- 0


# Loop for test each index
for (i in 1:length(ind)) {
    Best <- NbClust(data, diss = NULL, distance = "binary",
        min.nc = 2, max.nc = 5, method = "complete",
        index = ind[i])

    clusters[i] <- Best$Best.nc[1]
```

```
}
# Results
table(clusters)

clusters
1 2 3 4 5
1 4 2 3 8
```

We can try to use five clusters, and then make a visual validation to determine, if appropriate, by constructing a dendrogram:

```
# Load or Install packages for HClust
suppressWarnings(suppressMessages(if (!require(amap,
    quietly = TRUE)) install.packages("amap")))
library("amap")
# Model the Hierarchical Clustering
hclust <- hclusterpar(na.omit(dist(data), method = "euclidean",
link = "average", nbproc = 3))


# Generate a dendrogram plot.
# Load or Install packages for plotting
suppressWarnings(suppressMessages(if (!require(cba))
install.packages("cba")))
library("cba")
# Plotting Dendrogram
plot(hclust, main = "", sub = "", xlab = "")
title(main = "Cluster Dendrogram animals")
# Add in rectangles to show clusters.
rect.hclust(hclust, k = 5, border="blue")
```

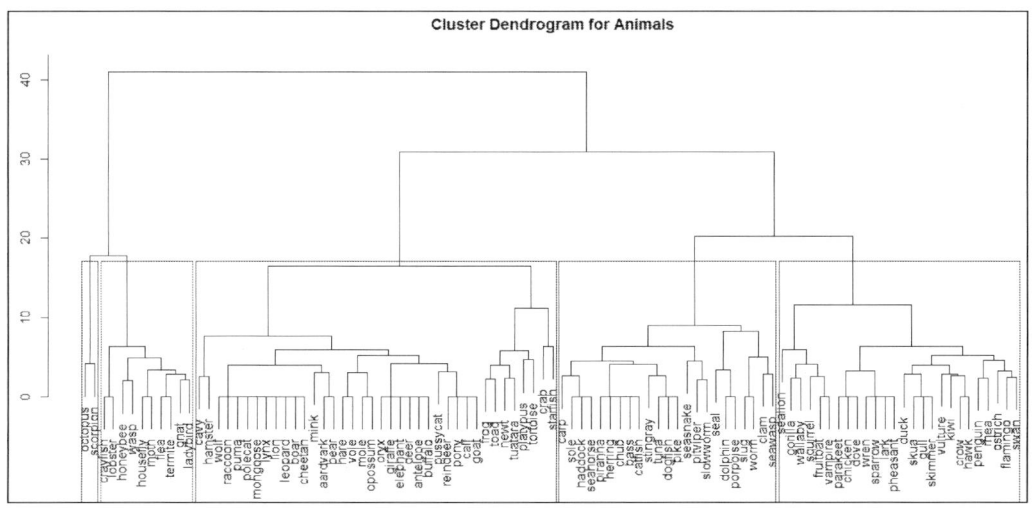

By using an agglomerative hierarchical clustering algorithm, we have classified the animals in the dataset based on the classification of 16 variables.

As you can see, in the preceding dendrogram, animals are grouped in a very coherent way, based on their characteristics.

 Dendrograms are tree structured charts used to visualize the result of a hierarchical clustering model. The result of a clustering is presented either as the distance or the similarity between the clustered rows or columns, depending on the selected distance measure.

Suppose now we want to make an analysis and we have validated the number of clusters for this analysis as five groups of animals. However, we do not have a classification done yet. What we did was cut five groups in the Dendrogram but only visually.

The information we've been working on in this example was stored in an object of type `data.frame` called `animals`. We will create a new column with the group number that corresponds to each animal:

```
# Cut dendrogram in K=5
group<-cutree(hclust, k = 5)

# Create a New data.frame with cluster

clusters<-(cbind(animals,group))

#Verify the cluster sizes
 table(clusters[17])


 1  2  3  4  5
38 23 26 10  2


# viewing some data

tail(clusters[12:17])
        fins legs tail domestic catsize group
vulture    0    2    1        0       1     3
wallaby    0    2    1        0       1     3
wasp       0    6    0        0       0     4
wolf       0    4    1        0       1     1
worm       0    0    0        0       0     2
wren       0    2    1        0       0     3
```

If you want to see some additional information of the clustering model that we built recently, you can use two functions that give us some interesting information.

For example, if we want to know what Centroids are suggested to our model of clustering according to each group and variable, we can use the `centers.hclust` function available in Togaware Rattle:

```
# List the suggested cluster centers for each cluster

suppressWarnings(
        suppressMessages(if
                              (!require(rattle, quietly=TRUE))
                    install.packages("rattle")))
library(rattle)
#Generate a matrix of centers from a hierarchical cluster.
centers<-as.data.frame(centers.hclust(animals, hclust, 5))
centers[1:5]
          hair   feathers       eggs       milk    airbone
1 0.81578947 0.0000000 0.2105263 0.8157895 0.0000000
2 0.04347826 0.0000000 0.8260870 0.1304348 0.0000000
3 0.23076923 0.7692308 0.7692308 0.2307692 0.6923077
4 0.40000000 0.0000000 1.0000000 0.0000000 0.6000000
5 0.00000000 0.0000000 0.5000000 0.0000000 0.0000000
```

The result is a matrix in which the left is the number of clusters and columns for each of the variables, with the centers suggested.

We can get more information about these clusters using the `fpc` package, specifically the `cluster.stats` function:

> `cluster.stats` returns a list object containing the components n, cluster.number, cluster.size, min.cluster.size, noisen, diameter, average.distance, median.distance, separation, average.toother, separation.matrix, average.between, average.within, n.between, n.within, within.cluster.ss, clus.avg.silwidths, avg.silwidth, g2, g3, pearsongamma, dunn, entropy, wb.ratio, ch, and corrected.rand.

A more detailed explanation can be consulted in the package help from R console:
help(cluster.stats).

```
suppressWarnings(
        suppressMessages(if
                            (!require(fpc, quietly=TRUE))
                install.packages("fpc")))
  cluster.stats(dist(animals), cutree(hclust, 5))
library("fpc")


$cluster.number
[1] 5
$cluster.size
[1] 38 23 26 10  2
$diameter
[1] 3.464102 3.000000 3.316625 2.645751 2.449490
$average.distance
[1] 1.602666 1.859203 1.848438 1.555814 2.449490
$median.distance
[1] 1.414214 2.000000 1.732051 1.732051 2.449490
$separation
[1] 1.000000 2.236068 2.000000 1.000000 2.236068
$average.toother
[1] 3.862762 4.579942 3.512338 4.577540 5.912404


$separation.matrix
          [,1]     [,2]     [,3]     [,4]     [,5]
[1,] 0.000000 4.000000 2.000000 1.000000 3.162278
[2,] 4.000000 0.000000 2.236068 6.000000 8.124038
[3,] 2.000000 2.236068 0.000000 4.358899 6.324555
[4,] 1.000000 6.000000 4.358899 0.000000 2.236068
[5,] 3.162278 8.124038 6.324555 2.236068 0.000000


$ave.between.matrix
          [,1]     [,2]     [,3]     [,4]     [,5]
[1,] 0.000000 4.757177 3.186985 3.379948 4.776153
[2,] 4.757177 0.000000 3.269283 6.559047 8.355525
[3,] 3.186985 3.269283 0.000000 4.700056 6.550575
[4,] 3.379948 6.559047 4.700056 0.000000 2.951741
[5,] 4.776153 8.355525 6.550575 2.951741 0.000000
```

The example shows just some of the statistics. The cluster.stats function may generate more.

Hierarchical clustering with factors

As mentioned in clustering techniques based on similarity and distance, these concepts are traditionally associated with numerical variables. Hence, clustering techniques are used for numeric variables.

However, it is very likely that, at some point, you will find a problem that ought to consider a qualitative variable. We will look at a way to do this directly in the R console in the following.

We will work with a new dataset, which is located in the following package of CRAN:

- **Package**: `ElemStatLearn`

- **Dataset**: SAheart: South African Hearth Disease Data

- **Description**:

  A retrospective sample of males in a high-risk heart-disease region of the Western Cape, South Africa.

- **Features**: `sbp` systolic blood pressure, `tobacco` cumulative tobacco (kg),`ldl` low density lipoprotein cholesterol, `adiposity` a numeric vector, `famhist` family history of heart disease, `type-A` behavior, `obesity` a numeric vector, `alcohol` current alcohol consumption, `age` at onset, `chd` response, coronary heart disease.

```
# Load dataset from package in CRAN
suppressWarnings(
        suppressMessages(if
                        (!require(ElemStatLearn))
                install.packages("ElemStatLearn")))
library("ElemStatLearn")
data(SAheart)
#Compactly Display the Structure
str(SAheart)

'data.frame': 462 obs. of  10 variables:
 $ sbp      : int  160 144 118 170 134 132 142 114 114 132 ...
 $ tobacco  : num  12 0.01 0.08 7.5 13.6 6.2 4.05 4.08 0 0 ...
 $ ldl      : num  5.73 4.41 3.48 6.41 3.5 6.47 3.38 4.59 3.83
 $ adiposity: num  23.1 28.6 32.3 38 27.8 ...
 $ famhist  : Factor w/ 2 levels "Absent","Present": 2 1 2 2 2
 $ typea    : int  49 55 52 51 60 62 59 62 49 69 ...
 $ obesity  : num  25.3 28.9 29.1 32 26 ...
 $ alcohol  : num  97.2 2.06 3.81 24.26 57.34 ...
 $ age      : int  52 63 46 58 49 45 38 58 29 53 ...
 $ chd      : int  1 1 0 1 1 0 0 1 0 1 ...
```

As can be seen, when we checked the structure of the dataset, it included a qualitative variable (factor). This variable is very important to identify the groups as it relates to family history of heart disease.

One solution might be to apply a transformation on this variable. However, we want to show a function to calculate a distance matrix. even in mixed dataset, the `daisy` function:

`daisy`: Computes all the pairwise distances between observations in the dataset. The original variables may be of mixed types. In that case, or whenever `metric = "gower"` is set, a generalization of Gower's formula. Also known as Gower's coefficient (1971), expressed as a dissimilarity. This implies that a particular standardization will be applied to each variable, and the `distance` between two units is the sum of all the variable specific distances:

```
# Distances Matrix
suppressWarnings(
        suppressMessages(if
                        (!require(cluster))
                install.packages("cluster")))
library("cluster")
diss<-suppressWarnings(daisy(SAheart, metric = "gower"))
```

With the statement above, we can create a distance matrix, which is stored in the `data.frame "diss"`, and we will use this to make a hierarchical clustering:

```
# Model the Hierarchical Clustering
suppressWarnings(h.factor <- hclusterpar(na.
omit(diss,method="complete", nbproc=3)))
plot(h.factor, hang = -1,main="Cluster Dendrogram")
rect.hclust(h.factor, k=4,border="blue")
```

Once we have validated the number of clusters with which we want to work, we proceed to integrate the original data and clusters in a new dataset:

```
#Insert the cluster number in a new dataset

group<-cutree(h.factor, k = 4)
Cluster<-cbind(SAheart,group)
table(Cluster$group)
```

Tips for choosing a hierarchical clustering algorithm

As we have seen, hierarchical clustering models have several different algorithms, and even though each has theoretical aspects that help to understand when it is convenient to use them, sometimes it may be easier just to check them all:

```
# Load or Install package dendextend
suppressWarnings(suppressMessages(if (!require(dendextend,
quietly =TRUE))install.packages("dendextend")))
library("dendextend")

# Load dataset Iris
data(iris)
Iris <- iris

# Create an object for storing dendrograms
irisdendlist <- dendlist()

# Vector with different link methods
methods <- c(
        "ward.D", "single", "complete", "average",
        "mcquitty", "median","centroid","ward.D2")
# Loop for create and store the 8 methods

for (i in seq_along(methods)) {
        hciris <- hclust(dist(Iris[1:4]), method = methods[i])
        irisdendlist <-
                dendlist(irisdendlist, as.dendrogram(hciris))
}

names(irisdendlist) <- methods

# Listing the dendrograms created irisdendlist
```

Using the preceding code, iteratively we create a hierarchical clustering model for each of the algorithms. These models are stored in an object similar to a list object containing the resulting dendrograms:

```
# listing the dendrograms created
        irisdendlist
$ward.D
'dendrogram' with 2 branches and 150 members total, at height
199.6205
```

```
$single
'dendrogram' with 2 branches and 150 members total, at height
1.640122
$complete
'dendrogram' with 2 branches and 150 members total, at height
7.085196
$average
'dendrogram' with 2 branches and 150 members total, at height
4.062683
$mcquitty
'dendrogram' with 2 branches and 150 members total, at height
4.497283
$median
'dendrogram' with 2 branches and 150 members total, at height
2.82744
$centroid
'dendrogram' with 2 branches and 150 members total, at height
2.994307
$ward.D2
'dendrogram' with 2 branches and 150 members total, at height
32.44761
```

Now, we can calculate the cophenetic correlation between each dendrogram created using `cor.dendlist`.

 The cophenetic correlation coefficient is a measure of how faithfully a dendrogram preserves the pairwise distances between the original unmodeled data points.

```
# Calculate the cophenetic correlation

cor <- round(cor.dendlist(irisdendlist), 2)

# Load or Install package corrplot
suppressWarnings(suppressMessages(if (!require(corrplot,
    quietly = TRUE)) install.packages("corrplot")))
library(corrplot)

# Plotting the correlations
col <- colorRampPalette(c("#BB4444", "#EE9988", "#FFFFFF",
    "#77AADD", "#4477AA"))
corrplot(cor, method = "shade", shade.col = NA, tl.col = "black",
    tl.srt = 45, col = col(200), addCoef.col = "black",
    order = "AOE")
```

As can be appreciated, considering the correlation factors, all methods are similar except for the **complete**. Considering their low correlation, we could discard **complete** and we can use a method with higher correlation.

We may also use the `fcb` package, in particular the `cluster.stats` function, to compare methods for various indices and decide which method is better. For example, the following code shows the comparison of three of them:

- `Within.cluster`: A generalization of the within clusters sum of squares (k-means objective function), which is obtained if d is a Euclidean distance matrix

- `Average.between`: Average distance between clusters

- `Average.within`: Average distance within clusters

```
# Load dataset Iris
data(iris)
Iris <- iris
# Make a distances matrix
dismatrix <- dist(Iris[1:4])

# Load or Install package fpc
suppressWarnings(suppressMessages(if (!require(fpc,
    quietly = TRUE)) install.packages("fpc")))
library("fpc")
```

```
# Vector with diferent link methods
methods <- c("ward.D", "single", "complete", "average",
    "mcquitty", "median", "centroid", "ward.D2")

# Loop for calculate the cluster stats
within.cluster <- 0
average.between <- 0
average.within <- 0

for (i in 1:length(methods)) {
    hciris <- hclust(dismatrix, method = methods[i])
    group <- cutree(hciris, k = 3)
    stats <- cluster.stats(dismatrix, group)

    within.cluster[i] <- stats$within.cluster.ss
    average.between[i] <- stats$average.between
    average.within[i] <- stats$average.within}

# Show results
data.frame(methods, within.cluster, average.between,
    average.within)
   methods within.cluster average.between average.within
1    ward.D       79.44538        3.400545       0.9296792
2    single      142.47937        4.008126       1.2728123
3  complete       89.52501        3.451052       1.0155770
4   average       79.44538        3.400545       0.9296792
5  mcquitty       79.54151        3.408377       0.9334433
6    median       86.96761        3.365954       0.9782928
7  centroid      142.47937        4.008126       1.2728123
8   ward.D2       79.29713        3.400042       0.9306286
```

Plotting alternatives for hierarchical clustering

Until now, we have not seen many alternatives for building graphs to represent HCA. However, there are some good options that allow us to go beyond the classic dendrograms.

A first resource that we can use is changing the chart settings in a traditional dendrogram:

```
# Load data from Iris file to R
Iris <- read.table("iris.csv", header = TRUE, sep = ",",
    dec = ".", row.names = 1)
# To make a reproducible Sample
```

```
set.seed(100)
ind <- sample(1:dim(Iris)[1], 50)
Sample <- iris[ind, ]
Sample$Species <- NULL
dismatrix <- dist(Sample)

# Build the clustering model
hciris <- hclust(dismatrix, method = "complete")
# plot dendrogram
plot(hciris, labels = Iris$Species[ind], col = "blue",
    col.main = "darkgreen", col.lab = "darkgreen",
    col.axis = "darkgreen", lwd = 2, lty = 3, sub = "",
    hang = -1, axes = FALSE)
# add Y axis
axis(side = 2, at = seq(0, 400, 100), col = "black",
    labels = FALSE, lwd = 2)
```

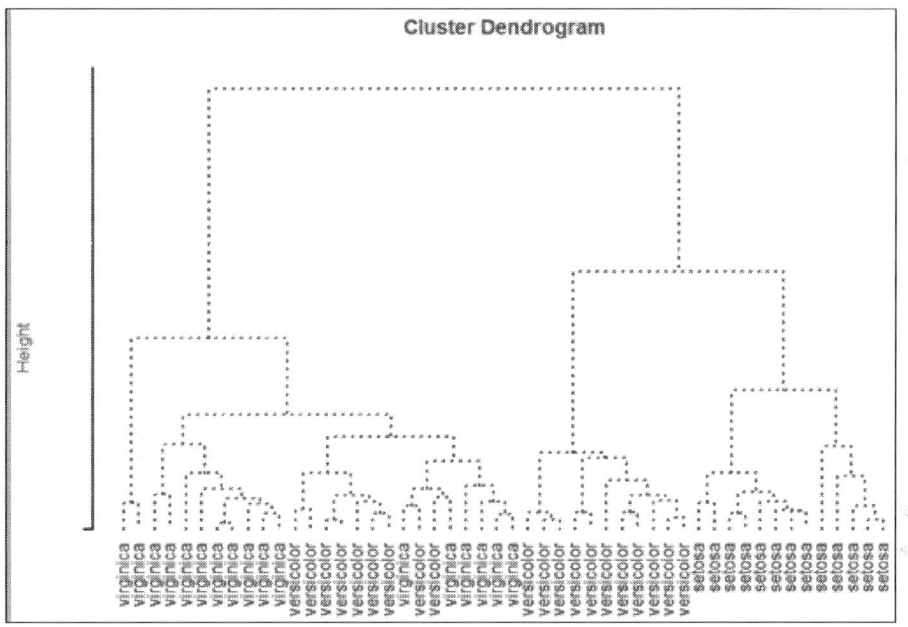

It is even possible to alter the shape of the nodes and the color of the labels in a dendrogram if we use the `dendrapply` function:

```
Iris <- read.table("iris.csv", header = TRUE, sep = ",",
    dec = ".", row.names = 1)
# To make a reproducible Sample
set.seed(100)
```

```
ind <- sample(1:dim(Iris)[1], 50)
Sample <- iris[ind, ]
Sample$Species <- NULL
dismatrix <- dist(Sample)

# Build the clustering model
hciris <- hclust(dismatrix, method = "complete")

# Set labels colors
labelColors <- c("#CDB380", "#036564", "#EB6841")

# cut dendrogram in 3 clusters
cluster <- cutree(hciris, 3)
hciris <- as.dendrogram(hciris)

# function to get color label
nodes <- function(n) {
    if (is.leaf(n)) {
        a <- attributes(n)
        labCol <- labelColors[cluster[which(names(cluster) ==
            a$label)]]
        attr(n, "nodePar") <- c(a$nodePar, lab.col = labCol)
    }
    n}

# Apply a Function to All Nodes of a Dendrogram
Dendro = dendrapply(hciris, nodes)

plot(Dendro, main = "New Dendrogram",type = "triangle")
```

Considering that a dendrogram is a representation based on a tree, you may also use a phylogenetic tree. This kind of chart is a branching diagram or *tree* showing the inferred evolutionary relationships among various entities.

One way to construct a Phylogenetic tree in R is using the package ape. This package provides functions for reading and manipulating phylogenetic trees and DNA sequences, computing DNA distances, estimating trees with distance-based methods, and a range of methods for comparative analyses and analysis of diversification. Functionalities are also provided for programming new phylogenetic methods.

The following is a possible implementation of the use of this package in R:

```
Iris <- read.table("iris.csv", header = TRUE, sep = ",",
    dec = ".", row.names = 1)
# To make a reproducible Sample
set.seed(100)
ind <- sample(1:dim(Iris)[1], 50)
Sample <- iris[ind, ]
Sample$Species <- NULL
dismatrix <- dist(Sample)

# Load or Install package ape
suppressWarnings(suppressMessages(if (!require(ape,
    quietly = TRUE)) install.packages("ape")))
library("ape")
# Build clustering model
hciris <- hclust(dismatrix, method = "complete")

# cutting dendrogram in 3 clusters
clusters = cutree(hciris, 3)

# Convert to phylo object
hciris <- as.phylo(hciris)
```

```
# Plot
color = c("red", "blue", "darkgreen")
plot(as.phylo(hciris), type = "fan", cex = log(Iris$Sepal.Width),
    tip.color = color[clusters])
```

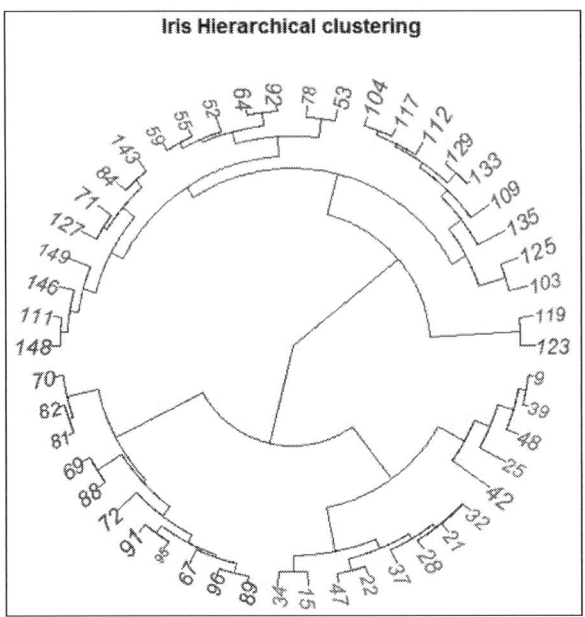

The preceding chart serves the same function as a dendrogram, showing the separation of observations hierarchically and identifying clusters.

We use two interesting tricks: Firstly, by the attribute `tip.color = color [clusters]`, we separate the color clusters and this is an important visual aid.

Secondly, we can play with the size of the headers, and as you may notice, the size of the numbers representing each observation is not the same for each. Using the attribute `cex = log (Iris $ Sepal.Width)` we tell R that the size of the labels will depend on the `Sepal.Width` variable, thus adding a new dimension to the graphic information.

Clustering by end-user interfaces

Using Toware Rattle, it is possible to cluster analysis without the need to interact directly with R. For that, you must have the data loaded and transformed into this tool, both of which were explained at the end of *Chapter 2, Working with Data: Exploratory Data Analysis*. So, we will avoid explaining that part again here. Then, we will see Rattle's clustering options:

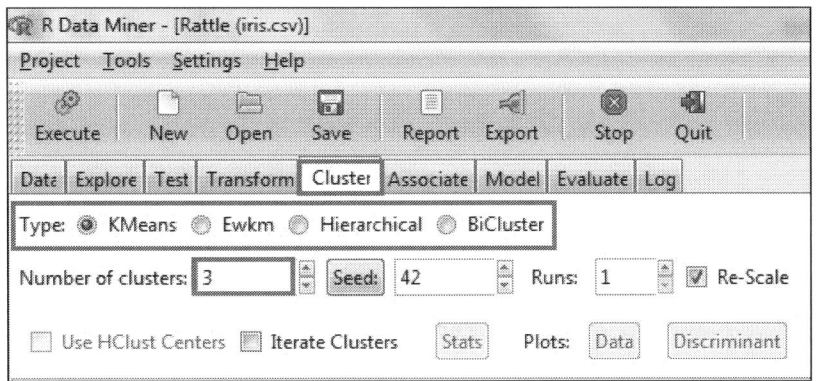

In the **Cluster** menu, simply select the **Type** label type clustering analysis that we require. In the preceding screenshot, we have chosen **K-Means**, and to do so, Rattle requires knowledge of the number of clusters. Considering that we are working with the Iris dataset, we choose three clusters and press the **Execute** button:

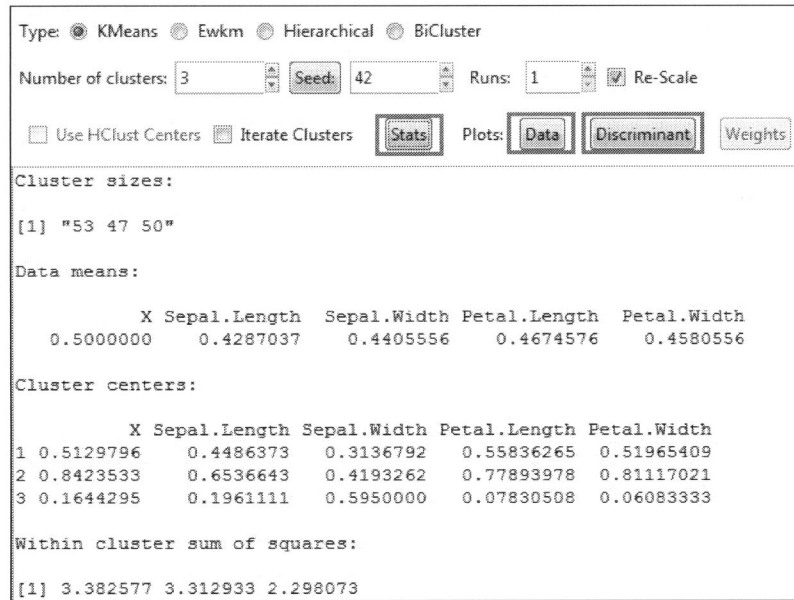

Rattle automatically generates some statistics of the clusters created, and if we press the **Data** or **Discriminant** buttons, it proceeds to generate some graphs of clusters created. In addition, the **Stats** button generates further details.

If, on the contrary, we want to work with hierarchical clustering, then, in the **Cluster** menu, select the **Hierarchical** option. We proceed to indicate the distance type we will use and the Linkage method, and finally click the **Execute** button:

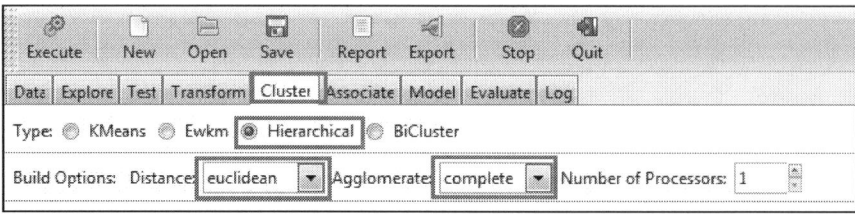

Rattle will proceed to automatically create a hierarchical clustering model:

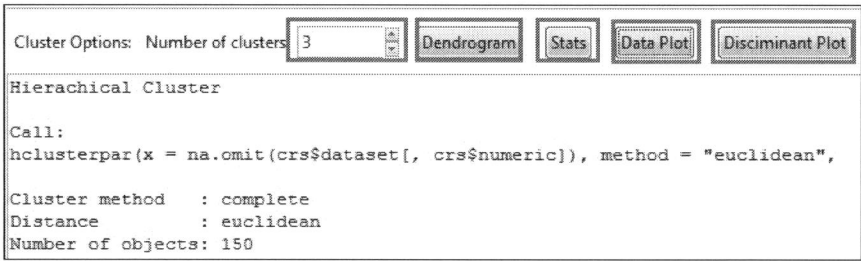

We can set the number of clusters that we see fit, and then pressing the **dendrogram** button, we will get a traditional dendrogram, or we can generate two additional charts using the **Plot Data** and **Discriminant Plot** button. Finally, we can also generate additional statistics for clusters created by the **Stats** button.

Finally, if we want to export these results, we can go through the **Evaluate** menu:

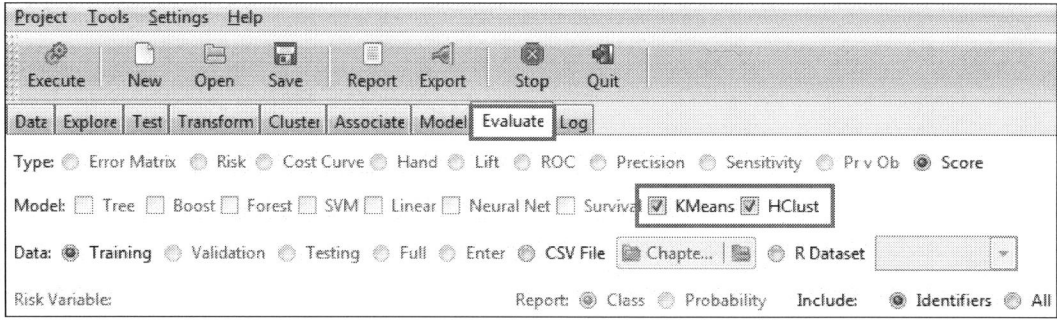

We check the options **K Means** and **hclust** and press the **Execute** button, and Rattle will assign to each observation in the dataset the cluster number according to the K-Means and according to the hierarchical clustering.

Summary

In this chapter, we explained what we consider relevant aspects in relation to one of the known techniques in unsupervised learning: cluster analysis.

We began by explaining the need to perform transformations in the data and some techniques to do so, and then we turned to the fundamental aspects of clustering analysis, starting with K-Means and ending with the hierarchical clustering.

Additionally, we provided an alternative for handling qualitative variables in mixed datasets, and some tips for choosing the appropriate algorithm as well as some options for plotting hierarchical clustering.

In the next chapter, we will learn about another grouping technique, the **association rules**. The association process makes groups of observations and attempts to discover links or associations between different attributes of group. These associations become rules that can, in turn, be used to support future decisions.

4

Association Rules

This chapter aims to explain another grouping technique, association rules. The association process makes groups of observations and attempts to discover links or associations between different attributes of groups. These associations become rules which can in turn be used to support future decisions.

Association rules can be applied in many situations but are commonly used in retail transactions. Its use became popular in selling books online. These businesses started to collect information about the reading habits of their customers and, using association analysis, they were able to identify groups of books that consumers with similar interests might buy.

These analyses allow us to create models of recommendation; one of the unsupervised learning techniques most commonly used today. For example, who is not familiar with some of these famous lines seen on major online stores?

"Your recently viewed items and featured recommendations…"

"Customers who bought this item also bought…"

"Frequently bought together…"

In this chapter, we will cover the following aspects:

- Fundamentals of association rules
- Representation
- Measures in association rules
- Exploring the association rules model
- Plotting alternatives
- Association rules by end-user tools

Fundamentals of association rules

In the context of data mining and machine learning, association rules are used to discover patterns that occur within a given dataset.

Association analysis identifies relationships between observations and variables from a dataset. These relationships are expressed by a set of rules that indicate groups of items that tend to be associated with others.

Usually, the association analysis is performed on large datasets, that is ones which contain a large number of registers, generally transactional, with at least one indicator to differentiate them, for example an invoice number.

Representation

In order to be able to identify relationships between items, it is necessary to use a system of representation for the rules. Suppose that in a dataset we have several sales transactions, each of these transactions consists of a set of sold items and every item sold in a transaction can be identified by a code, which in our example is a letter of the alphabet.

Considering the preceding information, a transaction of six articles could be represented as follows:

The purpose is to identify items that appear together in a number of transactions. Look at how a rule is built in a visual manner:

In the preceding figure, we can see a transaction of three items {A,C,F}. If we determine that there is a relationship between them, we can express it by an association rule of the form A,F è C and the interpretation would be as follows:

When the items **A** and **F** appear together in the same transaction, then typically, so does the item **C**.

Association rule models build a large number of these kinds of rules. As we saw, every rule is composed by two different sets of items, also known as itemsets, in the preceding example:

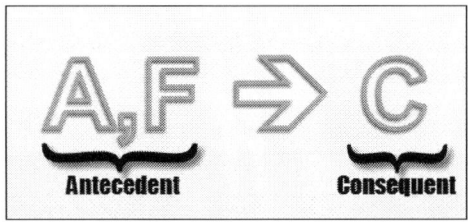

The rule can be divided into two parts, to the left would be the antecedent or LHS of the rule and at the right side the consequent or RHS of the rule.

Next, we develop an example of association rules directly in the R console, using the `arules` package. In the words of its author:

`arules`: Mining Association Rules and Frequent Itemsets

> *"It provides the infrastructure for representing, manipulating and analyzing transaction data and patterns (frequent itemsets and association rules). It also provides interfaces to C implementations of the association mining algorithms Apriori and Eclat."*

The data that we use in this example is included in the `arules` package.

The dataset contains one month's worth of real transaction data from a typical local grocery outlet. It contains 9835 transactions and 169 categories.

This dataset is provided for `arules` by Michael Hahsler, Kurt Hornik, and Thomas Reutterer.

```
#Loading or installing package arules
suppressWarnings(
        suppressMessages(if
                        (!require(arules, quietly=TRUE))
                install.packages("arules")))
library(arules)

#Loading data from arules package
data(Groceries)

Groceries
transactions in sparse format with
 9835 transactions (rows) and
 169 items (columns)
```

For the purposes of this example, the simplest way to load data is to call the dataset that will be used from the `arules` package as shown in the preceding code.

However, we will also make the load from a comma-separated file, since it requires a different instruction because it is a transaction dataset. In order to clarify the original shape of the dataset, we can see in the following, the first 10 transactions included in the original file, separated by commas:

```
1   citrus fruit,semi-finished bread,margarine,ready soups
2   tropical fruit,yogurt,coffee
3   whole milk
4   pip fruit,yogurt,cream cheese ,meat spreads
5   other vegetables,whole milk,condensed milk,long life bakery product
6   whole milk,butter,yogurt,rice,abrasive cleaner
7   rolls/buns
8   other vegetables,UHT-milk,rolls/buns,bottled beer,liquor (appetizer)
9   pot plants
10  whole milk,cereals
```

Now, we need to convert this data into a transaction dataset:

```
#Loading data from csv file
path<-"file:///C:/Unsupervised Learning/Chapter 04/Groceries.csv" #
Set your Path Here

Transactions<-read.transactions(path, sep = ",")

Transactions

transactions in sparse format with
 9835 transactions (rows) and
 169 items (columns)
```

We want to stress that the instruction to load data used earlier is different because `read.transactions` is a special instruction to load data from comma-separated files and convert them to the class `transactions`, which is the kind of data that we will require when working with models of association rules.

The `Transactions` class represents transaction data used to mine itemsets or rules. It is a direct extension of the class `itemMatrix` used to store a binary incidence matrix, item labels, and, optionally, transaction IDs and user IDs.

```
# verify the object's class
class(Transactions)
```

```
[1] "transactions"
attr(,"package")
[1] "arules"
```

Henceforth, we work with the data loaded from the comma-separated file, which is the `Transactions` object.

The object that stores data is of the kind `transactions`, which as we saw, is a special format to make associative analysis. Basically, it creates an object of the type list that contains spaces to store each transaction separately. On this object, we can make some initial exploratory analysis. For example, see the first five transactions loaded:

```
# List the first 5 transactions
inspect(Transactions[1:5])
   items
1 {citrus fruit,
   margarine,
   ready soups,
   semi-finished bread}
2 {coffee,
   tropical fruit,
   yogurt}
3 {whole milk}
4 {cream cheese ,
   meat spreads,
   pip fruit,
   yogurt}
5 {condensed milk,
   long life bakery product,
   other vegetables,
   whole milk}
```

Suppose we are not sure about the type of items that make up our work dataset, the next instruction can list the different items, which in our example are the products available. We observe how to list the top 10 products included:

```
# list the items of dataset
items<-as.data.frame(itemLabels(Transactions))
colnames(items) <- "Item"
head(items,10)

Item
1     abrasive cleaner
2     artif.sweetener
3     baby cosmetics
```

4	baby food
5	bags
6	baking powder
7	bathroom cleaner
8	beef
9	berries
10	beverages

It is also possible to generate a `summary` of the transaction file that we just created. This will give us some preliminary information:

```
> summary(Transactions)
transactions as itemMatrix in sparse format with
 9835 rows (elements/itemsets/transactions) and
 169 columns (items) and a density of 0.026

most frequent items:
      whole milk other vegetables        rolls/buns              soda              yogurt
          2513             1903             1809              1715                1372

element (itemset/transaction) length distribution:
sizes
   1    2    3    4    5    6    7    8    9   10   11   12   13   14   15   16   17
2159 1643 1299 1005  855  645  545  438  350  246  182  117   78   77   55   46   29
  21   22   23   24   26   27   28   29   32
  11    4    6    1    1    1    1    3    1

   Min. 1st Qu.  Median   Mean 3rd Qu.    Max.
      1       2       3      4       6      32

includes extended item information - examples:
          labels
1 abrasive cleaner
2 artif. sweetener
3   baby cosmetics
```

We can observe the most common items, such as the two most purchased items that are whole milk, appearing in 2513 purchases, and other vegetables, appearing in 1903 purchases. Another important fact is the size distribution of the itemsets. In this case, the number of items purchased in each transaction.

If we want to explore the frequency of some articles in specific, it is possible to extract some information individually. For example, suppose we want to consult the transactions ranging from 8 to 10 in the R console, in absolute amounts as well as in percentage terms of the total transactions:

```
# Check absolute and relative frequency

itemFrequency(Transactions[, 8:10],type = "absolute")

     beef   berries beverages
      516       327       256
```

```
round(itemFrequency(Transactions[, 8:10],type = "relative")*100,2)
    beef    berries beverages
    5.25      3.32      2.60
```

We can also produce a chart of frequencies and filter to consider only items with a minimum percentage of support or considering a `top` x of items, which is quite useful in analyzing the items that are most important in relation to their frequency:

```
# plot the frequency of items
par(mfrow = c(1, 2))

itemFrequencyPlot(Transactions, topN = 10,col="darkgreen")
itemFrequencyPlot(Transactions, support = 0.1,col="darkred")
```

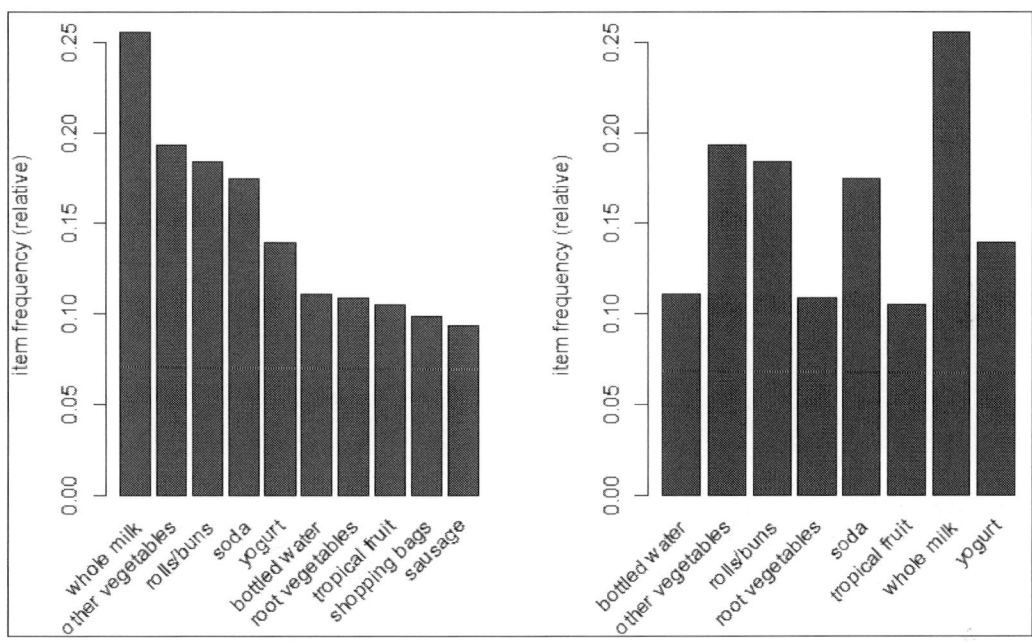

The chart on the left shows the top 10 most common items in the transactions dataset, while the chart on the right shows the items whose relative importance is at least 10%.

If we want to further explore the relationship between the different items of our transaction file, it is possible to calculate a distance matrix between them and even build a dendrogram to explore these relationships:

```
# Compute and returns distances for binary data in a matrix
x <- dissimilarity(Transactions, which = "items")
x[is.na(x)] <- 1 # get rid of missing values

# Hierarchical cluster analysis on a set of dissimilarities
hcd<-hclust(x)
par(mfrow = c(1, 1))
plot(hcd, cex=.6)
```

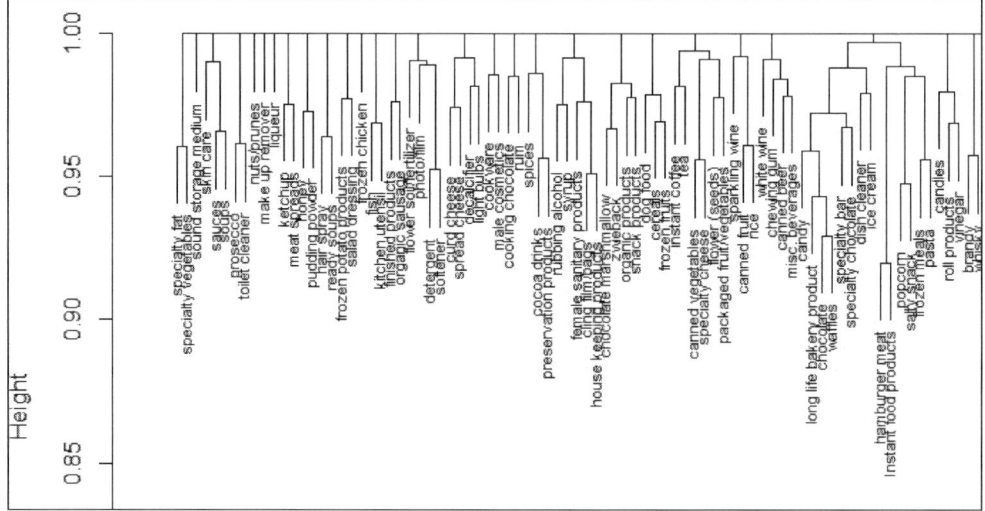

Given the size of the resulting dendrogram, for space-saving purposes the preceding figure is a part of the complete dendrogram.

Now that we have done some exploring on transactions, we will build a model based on association rules using the `apriori` function included in the `arules` package:

`apriori`: Mine frequent itemsets, association rules or association hyper edges using the Apriori algorithm. The Apriori algorithm employs level-wise search for frequent itemsets.

```
# Build apriori model with Min Support as 0.001
# and confidence as 0.8.
```

```
rules <- apriori (Transactions,
parameter = list(supp = 0.001, conf = 0.8))

rules
set of 410 rules
```

We have already created our model. However, at this point we will stop at the example in order to explain some important theoretical concepts relating to measures in association rules.

In these types of models, many rules are constructed. Hence, in order to achieve a greater benefit from them, we must use measures of significance and interest on the rules, determining which ones are interesting and which to discard.

The three most important measure parameters on an analysis of association rules are the support, the confidence and the lift:

Measure	Definition
Support	Defined as the proportion of transactions in the database which contain the itemset. How often the items appear together from amongst all of the transactions.
	Typically, we use small values for the support.
Confidence	It is a measure of how often one item X appears whenever another item Y appears in a transaction; it is a conditional probability:
	Confidence (X→Y) = P(Y | X) = P(X ∪ Y)/P(X)
	Typically, we use large values for confidence
Lift	Is the increased likelihood of X being in a transaction if Y is included in the transaction. If one rule had a lift of 1, it would imply that the probability of occurrence of the antecedent and that of the consequent are independent of each other. If the lift is > 1 it would imply that those two occurrences are dependent on one another and useful for predicting in future datasets

Returning to our example, we built the model using 0.001 Min Support and confidence as 0.8. With these parameters, we obtained 410 rules. However, in order to illustrate the sensitivity of the model to these two parameters, we will see what happens if we increase the support or lower the confidence level:

```
# Build apriori model with Min Support as 0.002
# and confidence as 0.8.
rules2 <- apriori (Transactions,
parameter = list(supp = 0.002, conf = 0.8))
```

```
# Build apriori model with Min Support as 0.002
and confidence as 0.6.
rules3 <- apriori (Transactions,
parameter = list(supp = 0.001, conf = 0.6))

rules2

set of 11 rules

rules3
set of 2918 rules
```

In the first case, we increase the minimum support of 0.001 to 0.002 and model rules went from 410 to only 11. In the other case we decrease the minimum confidence level to 0.6 and the number of model rules went from 410 to 2918. In the first case, using a high level of support can make the model lose interesting rules and in the second case, using a low confidence level increases the number of rules to quite an extent and many will not be useful.

The proper use of these two parameters greatly affects the outcome of the model rules of association, as it is very sensitive to both.

Exploring the association rules model

When we worked with the transaction file, we saw that it is stored in a special kind of object, which makes the models work in a similar way. This type of model is stored in a special object and its exploration also involves the use of specific commands.

Returning to our example, using the first version of the model, which we store in the rules object, we can perform an initial exploration by the summary function:

```
# Summary report of rules
summary(rules)

set of 410 rules

rule length distribution (lhs + rhs):sizes
   3   4   5   6
 29 229 140  12

   Min. 1st Qu.  Median   Mean 3rd Qu.    Max.
   3.0     4.0     4.0    4.3     5.0     6.0

summary of quality measures:
    support           confidence            lift
```

```
Min.    :0.00102    Min.    :0.80    Min.    : 3.1
1st Qu.:0.00102    1st Qu.:0.83    1st Qu.: 3.3
Median :0.00122    Median :0.85    Median : 3.6
Mean    :0.00125    Mean    :0.87    Mean    : 4.0
3rd Qu.:0.00132    3rd Qu.:0.91    3rd Qu.: 4.3
Max.    :0.00315    Max.    :1.00    Max.    :11.2


mining info:
          data transactions support confidence
  Transactions          9835    0.001        0.8
```

This function gives us information about the model that we built. For example, the size of rules, depending on the number of items that contain these rules. In this case, most of the rules have 3 and 4 items, but there are some rules that have up to 6. In addition, the summary model provides us with the main statistics related to the support, lift and confidence.

Although we know that our model has 410 rules, we still have not seen any. We can observe the rules that have been built and stored in the model. For example, we will extract the first 5 model rules:

```
# look at the first five rules

inspect(rules[1:5])


   lhs                    rhs              support confidence lift
1 {liquor,
   red/blush wine} => {bottled beer}   0.0019          0.90 11.2
2 {cereals,
   curd}           => {whole milk}     0.0010          0.91  3.6
3 {cereals,
   yogurt}         => {whole milk}     0.0017          0.81  3.2
4 {butter,
   jam}            => {whole milk}     0.0010          0.83  3.3
5 {bottled beer,
   soups}          => {whole milk}     0.0011          0.92  3.6
```

An interpretation of rule number one is: if someone buys liquor and red/blush wine, they are 90% likely to buy bottled beer too.

In the preceding code, we list the first 5 rules in the model. However, these rules are not ordered by any criteria of magnitude. Let's see how we can extract information ordered by some criteria such as the level of confidence:

```
# order rules by confidence

rules<-sort(rules, by="confidence", decreasing=TRUE)

# look at the first five rules

inspect(rules[1:5])

   lhs                          rhs             support confidence lift
1 {rice,
   sugar}                    => {whole milk}   0.0012          1   3.9
2 {canned fish,
   hygiene articles}         => {whole milk}   0.0011          1   3.9
3 {butter,
   rice,
   root vegetables}          => {whole milk}   0.0010          1   3.9
4 {flour,
   root vegetables,
   whipped/sour cream}       => {whole milk}   0.0017          1   3.9
5 {butter,
   domestic eggs,
   soft cheese}              => {whole milk}   0.0010          1   3.9
```

This time, the five rules we extracted from the model are ordered according to their level of confidence. In fact, the five rules have a confidence of 100. However, if we extract more rules, the confidence level will drop gradually.

If we want to sort the rules by other criteria such as lift or support, we only need to modify the previously used code indicating on the parameter by.

```
(by = "lift" or by = "support")
```

Another way we can interact with the model is generating subsets of specific rules, allowing us to do analysis on items of interest. For example, suppose we are particularly interested in making a promotion relating to the sale of yogurt, we could create a subset of rules concerning these products in this way:

```
# Subset the rules
# finding subsets of rules that precede yogurt purchases
yogurt <- subset(rules, subset = rhs %pin% "yogurt")
```

```
# Order by confidence
yogurt<-sort(yogurt, by="confidence", decreasing=TRUE)

# inspect top 5
 inspect(yogurt[1:5])

  lhs                       rhs        support confidence lift
1 {butter,
   cream cheese ,
   root vegetables}     => {yogurt}   0.0010        0.91  6.5
2 {butter,
   sliced cheese,
   tropical fruit,
   whole milk}          => {yogurt}   0.0010        0.91  6.5
3 {cream cheese ,
   curd,
   other vegetables,
   whipped/sour cream}  => {yogurt}   0.0010        0.91  6.5
4 {butter,
   other vegetables,
   tropical fruit,
   white bread}         => {yogurt}   0.0010        0.91  6.5
5 {pip fruit,
   sausage,
   sliced cheese}       => {yogurt}   0.0012        0.86  6.1
```

The preceding code shows us the items that the customers bought before purchasing yogurt. If we wished to verify the opposite situation, that is, what items the customers might buy who have previously bought yogurt, we only have to modify the code like this:

```
# Subset the rules
yogurt <- subset(rules, subset = lhs %pin% "yogurt")

# Order by confidence
yogurt<-sort(yogurt, by="confidence", decreasing=TRUE)

# inspect top 5
inspect(yogurt[15:19])
  lhs                       rhs            support confidence lift
1 {butter,
   domestic eggs,
   tropical fruit,
   yogurt}              => {whole milk}   0.0012        0.92  3.6
```

```
2 {cream cheese ,
   other vegetables,
   pip fruit,
   yogurt}                => {whole milk}  0.0011      0.92  3.6
3 {curd,
   domestic eggs,
   tropical fruit,
   yogurt}                => {whole milk}  0.0011      0.92  3.6
4 {butter,
   domestic eggs,
   root vegetables,
   yogurt}                => {whole milk}  0.0011      0.92  3.6
5 {domestic eggs,
   tropical fruit,
   whipped/sour cream,
   yogurt}                => {whole milk}  0.0011      0.92  3.6
```

An important point of these models is that they always have some level of redundancy, that is, rules that mean the same for the purposes of analysis. One way to deal with them is to simply exclude them, which can be done from the console as follows:

```
# Subset and delete redundants
subset <- is.subset(rules, rules)
subset[lower.tri(subset, diag=T)] <- NA
redundant <- colSums(subset, na.rm=T) >= 1
pruned <- rules[!redundant]
rules.pruned<-pruned

rules
set of 410 rules

rules.pruned
set of 330 rules
```

Following the preceding procedure, 80 rules which are redundant are located and excluded.

Plotting alternatives for association rules

Although the rules are easy to interpret without using graphical tools, it is sometimes interesting to use visual tools. A very good package to plot models based on the analysis of association rules is `arulesViz` because it has a variety of specialized graphics.

`arulesViz`: For help visualizing association rules and frequent itemsets there is an `Extends` package for `arules` with various visualization techniques for association rules and itemsets. The package also includes several interactive visualizations for rule exploration.

Let's see how we can build a map of rules in R:

```
#Loading or installing package arulesViz
suppressWarnings(
        suppressMessages(if
                        (!require(arulesViz, quietly=TRUE))
                install.packages("arulesViz")))
library(arulesViz)
rules <- apriori(Transactions, parameter = list(supp = 0.001,
conf = 0.8))
rules<-sort(rules, by="confidence", decreasing=TRUE)
# Subset and delete redundants
subset <- is.subset(rules, rules)
subset[lower.tri(subset, diag=T)] <- NA
redundant <- colSums(subset, na.rm=T) >= 1
pruned <- rules[!redundant]
rules.pruned<-pruned
plot(rules.pruned[1:10],method="graph",interactive=TRUE))
```

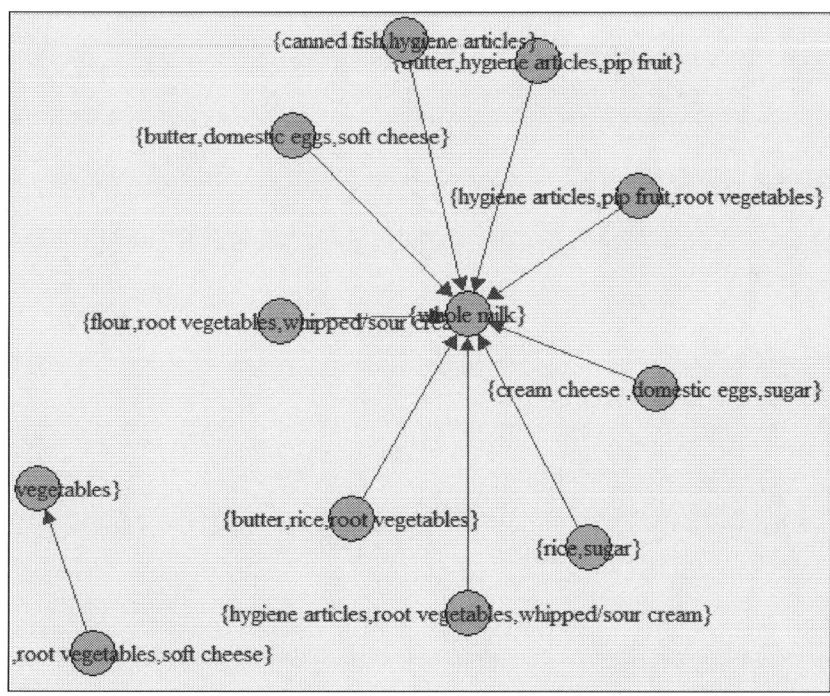

Association rules by end-user tool

To this point, we have explored models based on association rules using R console. However, we consider it appropriate to mention an alternative that does not require using the console directly.

To do this, we will again use the togaware rattle. It can be loaded by the following instruction:

```
# Set language to English
Sys.setenv(LANGUAGE="en")
#Load Rattle Package
suppressWarnings(suppressMessages(library(rattle)))
# Load visual interface
rattle()
```

The data is loaded from the **Data** menu, and we proceed to use the file selector and seek the dataset **Groceries that** we have been using:

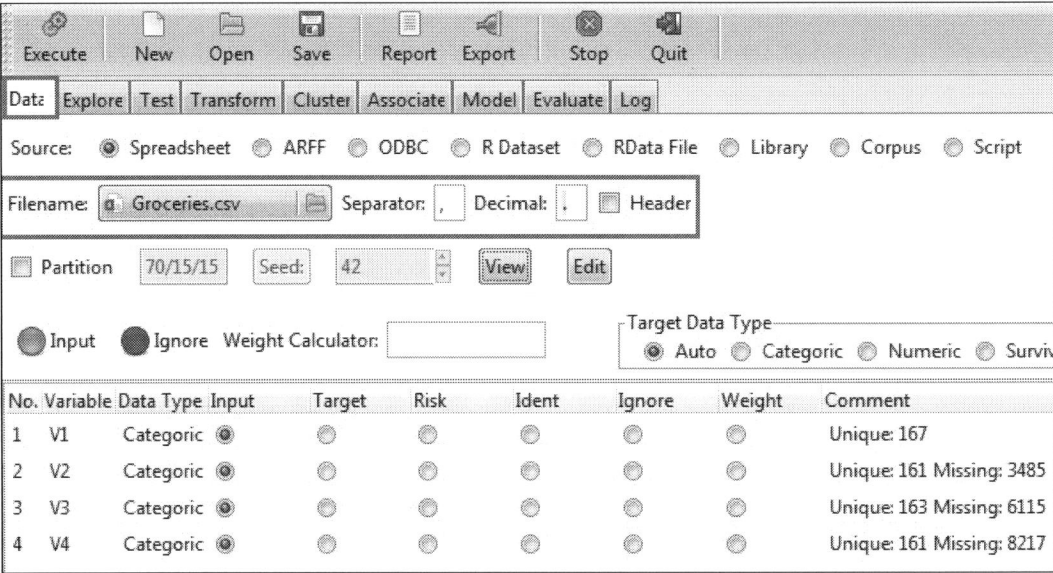

Once you have loaded the data, we access the **Associate** menu and indicate a level of support of 0.001 and a minimum confidence level of 0.8 and press the **Execute** button:

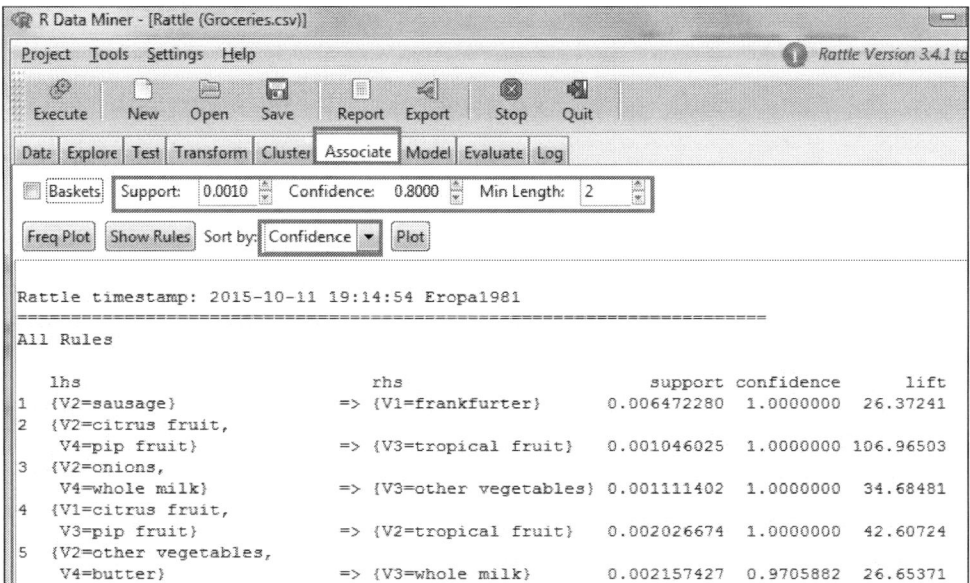

The rattle builds the model a priori, along with association rules. However, the exploration we can do with this tool is very limited.

Summary

In this chapter, we went through the aspects that we considered relevant in relation to models based on association rules; one of the techniques more broadly known in the field of unsupervised learning and perhaps one of the pillar techniques in data mining.

We started with the theoretical foundations, their representation, and some measures that we know for proper application. Later, we built a model in R and explored the specialized functions for it. You learned how to navigate the model, eliminate redundant rules, and work with rules on segments of interest. We illustrated the use of packages to graph models based on rules and, finally, we mentioned an alternative type of end-user interface for working with association rules models.

In the next chapter, we will study the concept of dimensionality reduction and its importance in building models for unsupervised learning.

5
Dimensionality Reduction

This chapter aims to explain some dimensionality reduction techniques in machine learning. This concept refers to the process of reducing the number of random variables considered and can be subdivided in feature selection and feature extraction. The key is to reduce the number of dimensions, while preserving most parts of the information.

In this chapter, we will cover feature extraction techniques, while feature selection will be approached in the next chapter.

These kinds of techniques aim to solve the problem of dimensionality, which refers to the inconveniences associated with multivariate data analysis when the dimensionality, that is the number of variables, is too large.

The problem of dimensionality implies that, given a fixed number of cases, there is a maximum number of attributes beyond which the efficiency of models is degraded rather than improved. In the knowledge discovery process, *more is not always better*, and this often gives better results focused on a few variables that explain most of the information that will answer our problem.

In this chapter, we will cover the following aspects:

- The problem of high dimensionality
- Alternatives to mitigate the effects of the curse of dimensionality
- **Principal Component Analysis** (**PCA**): Concept construction and graphical analysis
- Hierarchical clustering on PCA
- PCA by user interfaces

The curse of dimensionality

The curse of dimensionality, sometimes referred to as the Hughes effect, is a term often used to refer to the phenomena occurring in mathematics and statistics, when we try to analyze and organize data in multidimensional spaces.

These phenomena occur in various fields including numerical analysis, combinatory sampling, machine learning, and data mining. They have a common cause: when the dimensionality increases, the volume of space increases exponentially, causing the available data to become scattered; this is problematic for any method that requires statistical significance. The reason for this is that the result to be statistically significant as the variables increase, the required data grows exponentially.

For example, in the context of machine learning, the curse of dimensionality can mean a serious inconvenience in solving problems that involve optimization or use of distances, as these tend to grow with increasing dimensionality, that is, data is increasingly more dispersed. This implies that when the number of dimensions increases, finding "things" or measuring their size and shape becomes increasingly complex.

Suppose we have a clustering problem, as discussed in *Chapter 3, Identifying and Understanding Groups: Clustering Algorithms*, and we want to group them by their distances. Imagine a square that represents the 2D feature space, the features that we will use to group together. The average of this space is the center of the square, and all observations are inside a circle that is inscribed in the square.

The observations that do not fall within this circle are closer to the corners of the search space than to its center. This observation is like an outlier and it is hard to group them in clusters. Clustering is easier if most observations fall inside the inscribed circle:

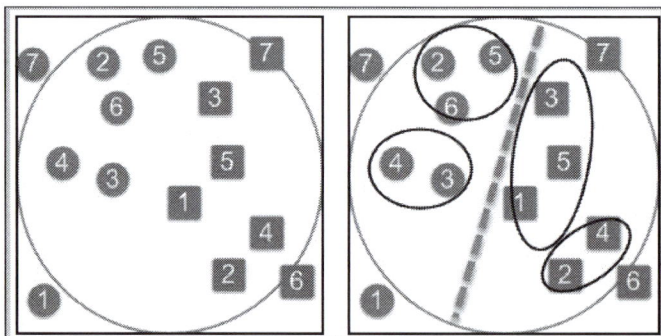

On the left we can see the square, circle, and observations before a cluster analysis and to the right we see a possible result of grouping observations.

Now, the preceding example is based on a two-dimensional space, but let's see what would happen if both the square and the circle coexist in a plane of higher dimensionality.

By increasing the dimension of the square, it becomes an n-dimensional hypercube. Furthermore, the circle becomes an n-dimensional hypersphere. The hypersphere has a very interesting behavior that helps us better understand the curse of dimensionality.

The volume of the inscribed hypersphere of dimension d and with radius 0.5 can be calculated with the following formula:

$$V(d) = \frac{\pi^{d/2}}{\Gamma(\frac{d}{2}+1)} 0.5^d$$

We will proceed to calculate the volume in several dimensions to observe the effect of increasing the dimensionality. For ease, we can do it directly in the R console, using the package *SphericalCubature*.

In the words of its author:

> "*SphericalCubature is a package that defines several methods to integrate functions over the unit sphere and ball in n-dimensional Euclidean space. Routines for converting to/from multivariate polar/spherical coordinates are also provided.*"

```
# Loading or installing package 'SphericalCubature'
suppressWarnings(suppressMessages(if (!require(SphericalCubature,
    quietly = TRUE)) install.packages("SphericalCubature")))
library(SphericalCubature)
# Set radius to 0.5
r <- 0.5

# 20 Dimensions Loop
Dimensions = rep(0, 20)
SphereVol <- Dimensions
for (k in 0:20) {
    n <- k

    SphereVol[k] = ballVolume(k - 1, R = r)
}
```

```
plot(SphereVol, col = "blue", type = "b", ylab = "volume of the
hypersphere",
    xlab = "Dimensions")
```

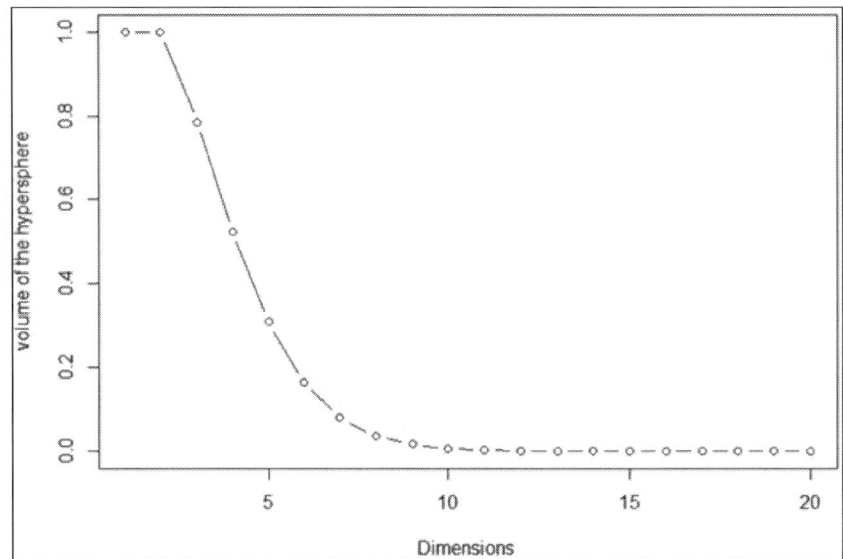

The preceding figure shows how the volume of the hypersphere changes when the dimensionality increases and tends to reach zero; as the dimensionality tends to reach infinity, the hypersphere shrinks to insignificance. For this reason, distance metrics start losing their effectiveness in measuring the dissimilarity in highly dimensional spaces.

In general, data mining algorithms tend to degrade in performance and usefulness as dimensionality increases.

Feature extraction

Dimensionality reduction includes a set of techniques to help deal with the problem of the curse of dimensionality. These techniques are aimed at reducing the number of variables to be considered by the models we build, generally falling into feature selection and feature extraction.

In the context of machine learning, the term *feature extraction* is associated with techniques that seek to build a dataset derived and transformed from the original data.

One of the best known and most used techniques to reduce the dimensionality is Principal Components Analysis or PCA.

Principal component analysis

Principal component analysis (PCA) is a technique to reduce the dimensionality of a dataset, in fact, it is one of the most well known and widely used. This technique finds the causes that explain the variability of a dataset and lists them in the order of their importance.

The PCA searches for a projection where the data is best represented in terms of the least squares. It performs a linear transformation to obtain a new coordinate system in which the largest variance is considered as the principal component, the second largest variance as the second principal component, and so on.

New components are not specified in the original measurement units as they are a linear combination of the original variables. Moreover, the PCA eliminates the correlations between them, while the new variables, that are the principal components, are independent from one another.

An advantage of principal component analysis as a dimensionality reduction method is that it preserves the characteristics of the dataset that contribute most to its variance. Another advantage connected with reduced dimensions is that the behavior of the dataset is easier to observe in 2D and 3D systems, which makes it more interpretable by humans.

In general terms, there are two ways in which you can calculate the principal components:

- **Using a correlation matrix**: for data which is not dimensionally uniform about the magnitude of the variables.
- **Using a covariance matrix**: for data that is dimensionally uniform about the magnitude of the variables and have similar mean values.

Even though the mathematical aspects of the technique are interesting, explaining it in depth is beyond the scope of this book, which has a more applied approach.

However, we are interested in the general understanding of the technique and its application. Therefore, we will develop an example to clarify the importance of principal component analysis and how we can use R to perform this analysis.

In this example, we use data about the performance of some students in five classes: Maths, Science, English, History, and Sports. Each of these subjects is as a dimension, that is, we will work with a dataset of five dimensions:

	5 Dimensions				
Student	**Maths**	**Science**	**English**	**History**	**Sports**
Rosa	7	6,5	9,2	8,6	8
Denis	7,5	9,4	7,3	7	7
Edgar	7,6	9,2	8	8	7,5
Yeison	5	6,5	6,5	7	9
Silvia	6	6	7,8	8,9	7,3
Arturo	7,8	9,6	7,7	8	6,5
Elizabeth	6,3	6,4	8,2	9	7,2
Erik	7,9	9,7	7,5	8	6
Dante	6	6	6,5	5,5	8,7
Sasha	6,8	7,2	8,7	9	7

(10 Observations)

For didactic purposes, we decided to use few observations, and we will work with the qualifications of 10 students in the aforementioned subjects.

As always, the first thing to do is to load the data from the source to an R console:

```
# Principal Components Example: Students Performance

# Load the data

# Set your Path Here:

path <- "file:///C:/Unsupervised Learning/Students.csv"

Students <- read.csv(path, sep = ";", dec = ",", na.strings = c(".",
    "NA", "", "?"), strip.white = TRUE, encoding = "UTF-8",
    row.names = 1)
```

```
        Maths Science English History Sports
Rosa      7.0    6.5     9.2    8.6    8.0
Denis     7.5    9.4     7.3    7.0    7.0
Edgar     7.6    9.2     8.0    8.0    7.5
Yeison    5.0    6.5     6.5    7.0    9.0
Silvia    6.0    6.0     7.8    8.9    7.3
Arturo    7.8    9.6     7.7    8.0    6.5
```

```
Elizabeth    6.3    6.4    8.2    9.0    7.2
Erik         7.9    9.7    7.5    8.0    6.0
Dante        6.0    6.0    6.5    5.5    8.7
Sasha        6.8    7.2    8.7    9.0    7.0
```

Once we have the data loaded into R, we can run a principal component analysis on quantitative variables in the dataset, along the example. We will show various ways to do so and we will use different packages to offer a wide range of alternatives.

To better understand what happens when we make the principal component analysis in R, we can observe the following chart:

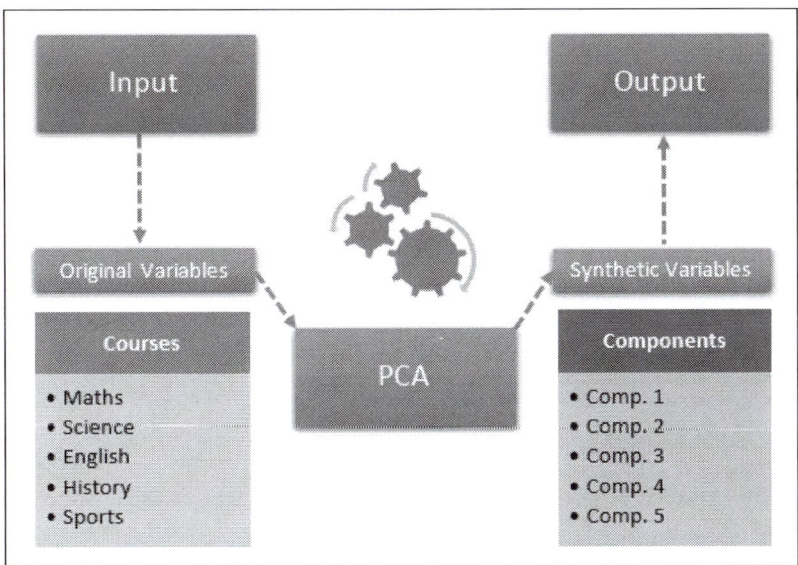

The input variables are the results of students in each of the subjects mentioned above, that is the original variables. When you run the PCA, changes will take place in the input data and synthetic variables are created. These new variables are the components that will be the model output.

We will calculate the principal components by two approaches: The SVD or Singular value decomposition (preferred for numeric accuracy) and by an alternative approach to determine the eigenvalues of the covariance matrix.

Continuing the example, we will use, as first choice, the princomp function integrated in the stats package.

In the words of its author:

> "*princomp performs a principal components analysis on the given numeric data matrix and returns the results as an object of class "princomp". The calculation is done using eigens on the correlation or covariance matrix.*"

```
# Principal Components Analysis using princomp
PCA <- princomp(na.omit(Students), scale = TRUE, center = TRUE,
tol = 0)

# Check the created object

PCA
Call:
princomp(x = na.omit(Students), scale = TRUE, center = TRUE,
    tol = 0)

Standard deviations:
    Comp.1     Comp.2     Comp.3     Comp.4     Comp.5
1.87037681 1.33918427 0.52039936 0.38878066 0.08780771

 5  variables and  10 observations.
```

Generally, the PCA results should consist of a set of eigenvalues, the principal components, and a matrix with loadings or correlations between variables and these components.

Using the eigenvalues, we can get information about the variability in the dataset. The scores give us information about the structure of the observations, and the loadings or correlations allow you to get a sense of the relationships between variables, as well as their associations with the extracted principal components.

Let's see how we can obtain this information on the console:

```
# loadings for first 3 components

unclass(PCA$loadings[,1:3])
                 Comp.1     Comp.2      Comp.3
Maths      -0.4554991 -0.0301873  0.47296282
Science    -0.7730822  0.3366382 -0.04147109
English    -0.1117975 -0.5349732  0.62844982
History    -0.1416005 -0.7479026 -0.35163283
Sports      0.4028835  0.2005213  0.50595602

# Principal Components aka scores (first 3 components)
```

```
PCA$scores[,1:3]
                 Comp.1      Comp.2       Comp.3
Rosa         0.76471745  -1.5817637   1.11186219
Denis       -1.66887794   1.3919656   0.09067929
Edgar       -1.57822841   0.2994960   0.48752985
Yeison       2.60701317   1.3202040  -0.46230941
Silvia       1.43877557  -1.3356687  -0.67985389
Arturo      -2.34790534   0.3880845  -0.12895699
Elizabeth    0.89372557  -1.5189012  -0.38893244
Erik        -2.64984571   0.4254636  -0.46447580
Dante        2.62959083   2.1833951   0.40705140
Sasha       -0.08896518  -1.5722752   0.02740580
```

Something very important to note is that we can generate information about the importance of the principal components:

```
summary(PCA)
Importance of components:
                        Comp.1 Comp.2 Comp.3 Comp.4 Comp.5
Standard deviation       1.870  1.339  0.5203 0.3887 0.0878
Proportion of Variance   0.611  0.313  0.0473 0.0264 0.0013
Cumulative Proportion    0.611  0.924  0.9722 0.9986 1.0000
```

As we can see in the preceding table, the cumulative proportion of variance accounted for each component reaching 92% in the second component.

This means that 92% of the behavior of the dataset is now explained in component 1 and component 2, while the other components can be easily discarded from the analysis without much loss of information.

Now, if we want to minimize the loss of information, we could work with the first 3 components, which would achieve 97% representation of the data.

It is possible to evaluate the quality of the representation of the principal components to determine which accounts for the largest amount of information:

```
# Display a plot showing the relative importance of the components.

plot(PCA, main="",col="darkgreen")
title(main="Principal Components Importance for Students")
```

As shown in the following graph, the first two components are those that explain most of the variance of the dataset:

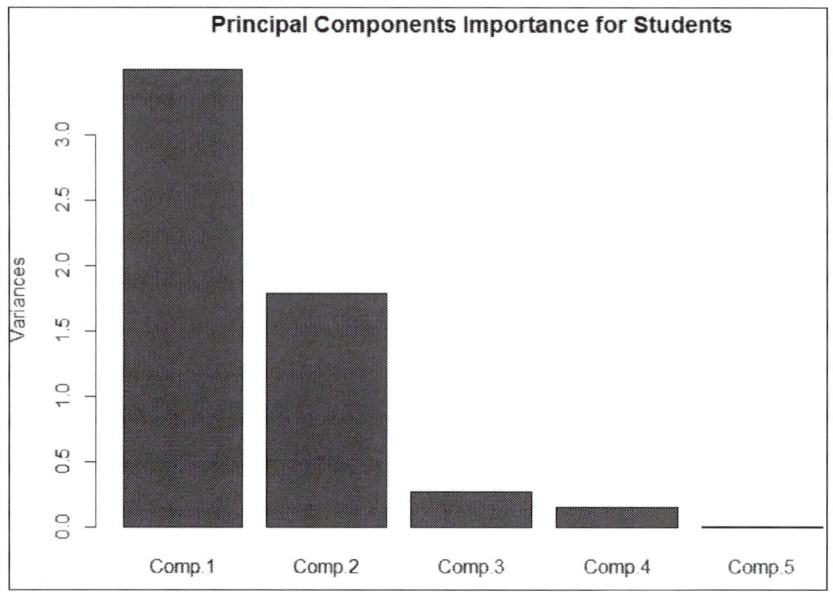

Whether principal component analysis is well suited to the data being analyzed, that is whether the first components collect enough information, is something you can represent graphically.

For graphical presentation of principal components, there are several options. We will use the first alternative, biplots:

A `biplot` is an enhanced use of a scatterplot, both points and vectors, to represent structure. The axes of a biplot are a pair of main components. These axes are drawn in black and are labeled PC1, and PC. Let's see how to build a biplot on R:

```
# Display a plot showing the two principal
# components Set the components to plot
components <- c(1, 2)

# Plot
biplot(PCA, main = "", choices = components)
title(main = "Principal Components Analysis for Students")
```

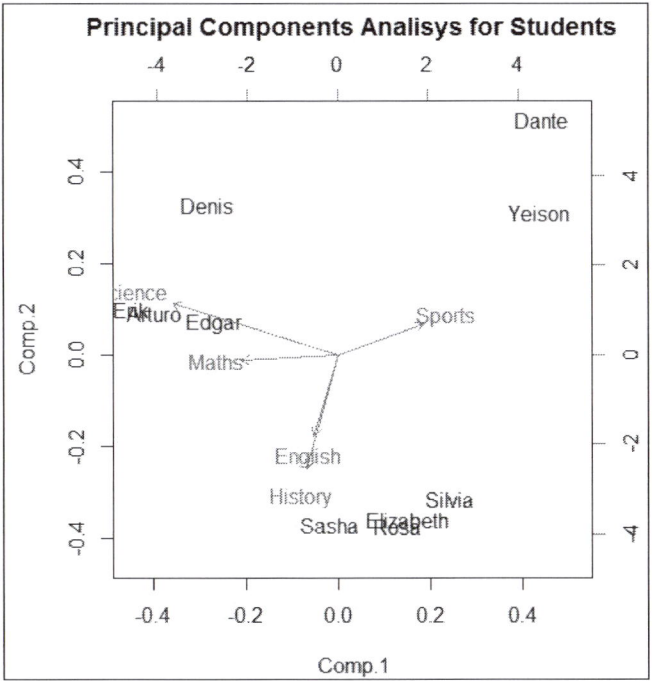

Biplots are useful charts in multivariate representations. The prefix *bi* refers to the overlap of individuals and variables in the same representation. Individuals are represented as points in the plane and variables are shown as arrows with respect to the axes. The interpretation of a `biplot` is based on simple geometric concepts, such as the angles between the variables representing its correlation, and distance between individuals representing their similarity.

As we mentioned when using the function `princomp`, the calculation is done using Eigen on the correlation or covariance matrix. If we want to take a different approach, it is possible using SVD, using the `prcomp` function.

In the words of its author:

> *"prcomp performs a principal components analysis on the given data matrix and returns the results as an object of class "prcomp". The calculation is done by a singular value decomposition of the (centered and possibly scaled) data matrix, not by using eigen on the covariance matrix. This is generally the preferred method for numerical accuracy."*

As an alternative to the `princomp` function, you can use the function `prcomp`. Actually, the use of both are very similar. Let's look at how to do it in the console of R:

```
# Load the data

path<-"file:///C:/Unsupervised Learning/Students.csv" # Set your
Path Here

Students<-read.csv(path, sep=";", dec=",", na.strings=c(".", "NA",
"", "?"),strip.white=TRUE, encoding="UTF-8", row.names=1)

Students

# Principal Components Analysis using prcomp
PCA2 <- prcomp(na.omit(Students), scale=TRUE,        center=TRUE,
tol=0)

#Check the created object
PCA2

Standard deviations:
[1] 1.70095552 1.27618589 0.58872409 0.35016062 0.09429419

 # Principal Components Analysis using prcomp
 PCA2 <- prcomp(na.omit(Students), scale=TRUE, center=TRUE, tol=0)

 # Check the created object
 PCA2
Standard deviations:
[1] 1.70095552 1.27618589 0.58872409 0.35016062 0.09429419
Rotation:
            PC1       PC2       PC3       PC4      PC5
Maths   -0.5266 -0.27049  0.43820 -0.26121 -0.6238
Science -0.4249 -0.50807  0.04049  0.67362  0.3253
English -0.3591  0.56208  0.56227 -0.07008  0.4837
History -0.3526  0.58648 -0.39418  0.44664 -0.4204
Sports   0.5373  0.09374  0.57862  0.52305 -0.3067

# Summarizes the importance of the components found.

summary(PCA2)
Importance of components:
                         PC1    PC2    PC3     PC4     PC5
Standard deviation    1.7010 1.2762 0.58872 0.35016 0.09429
Proportion of Variance 0.5786 0.3257 0.06932 0.02452 0.00178
Cumulative Proportion  0.5786 0.9044 0.97370 0.99822 1.00000
```

Considering that the two graphs viewed for PCA are implemented by the `princomp` function, apply them in the same way for the `prcomp` function, and we will not repeat them here.

If we go a little beyond the basic packages that are installed with R, we can choose to use `FactoMineR`. This is a highly recommended package for multivariate exploratory analysis in general. In fact, it is my favorite because it creates more explanatory graphics.

`FactoMineR`: Multivariate exploratory data analysis and data mining with R. The methods proposed in this package are exploratory multivariate methods, such as principal component analysis, correspondence analysis, or clustering.

Using the data from the student example, we will create a principal components analysis, this time using the PCA function from the package `FactoMiner`.

PCA: Performs **Principal Component Analysis (PCA)** with supplementary individuals, supplementary quantitative variables, and supplementary categorical variables.

Here is an implementation directly on the console of R:

The first thing to do is install the package and load the data that we will use:

```
#Loading or installing package "FactoMiner"
suppressWarnings(
        suppressMessages(if
                        (!require(FactoMineR, quietly=TRUE))
                install.packages("FactoMineR")))
library(FactoMineR)

# Load dataset students
path<-"file:///C:/Unsupervised Learning/Students.csv" # Set your
Path Here
Students <- read.table(path, header=TRUE,
  sep=";", na.strings="NA", dec=",", row.names=1, strip.white=TRUE)

Students.PCA<-Students[, c("Maths", "Science", "English",
  "History",
  "Sports")]
```

Once we have loaded the data, we can generate the principal component analysis using the PCA function included in the package `FactoMiner`:

```
# Build the PCA in FactoMiner
res<-PCA(Students.PCA , scale.unit=TRUE, ncp=5, graph = FALSE)

res

**Results for the Principal Component Analysis (PCA)**
The analysis was performed on 10 individuals, described by 5 variables

*The results are available in the following objects:

   name                    description
1  "$eig"                  "eigenvalues"
2  "$var"                  "results for the variables"
3  "$var$coord"            "coord. for the variables"
4  "$var$cor"              "correlations variables - dimensions"
5  "$var$cos2"             "cos2 for the variables"
6  "$var$contrib"          "contributions of the variables"
7  "$ind"                  "results for the individuals"
8  "$ind$coord"            "coord. for the individuals"
9  "$ind$cos2"             "cos2 for the individuals"
10 "$ind$contrib"          "contributions of the individuals"
11 "$call"                 "summary statistics"
12 "$call$centre"          "mean of the variables"
13 "$call$ecart.type"      "standard error of the variables"
14 "$call$row.w"           "weights for the individuals"
15 "$call$col.w"           "weights for the variables"
```

One of the many qualities of `FactoMiner` is that it provides much information in the preceding code. We proceeded to build a PCA and store the results in an object called `res`. This object is very special, as its type is PCA - List, which means that our models are stored inside with 15 additional elements of information. Some of the most important are:

Name in list of results	Includes
`eig`	A matrix containing all the eigenvalues, the percentage of variance and the cumulative percentage of variance
`var`	A list of matrices containing all the results for the active variables (coordinates, correlation between variables and axes, square cosine, contributions)

Name in list of results	Includes
ind	A list of matrices containing all the results for the active individuals (coordinates, square cosine, contributions)
call	A list with a summary of statistics

Let's see how this information can be accessed from the console of R:

```
# getting information from PCA Model

# Matrix containing all the eigenvalues
res$eig
           eigenvalue        % variance cum.        % variance
comp 1    2.893249673      57.8649935             57.86499
comp 2    1.628650425      32.5730085             90.43800
comp 3    0.346596049       6.9319210             97.36992
comp 4    0.122612460       2.4522492             99.82217
comp 5    0.008891393       0.1778279            100.00000
```

The eigenvalues correspond to the amount of the variation explained by each principal component. They are large for the first component and small for the subsequent components.

A component with an eigenvalue greater than 1 indicates that the component accounts for more variance than accounted for by one of the original variables in the standardized data. This can be used as a cutoff point to determine the number of principal components to retain.

Looking at the cumulative variance, the results are similar with respect to those found with the above packages. In the second principal component, 90% of the explained variance is reached and 97% in the third. If we prefer to observe it graphically, we can build a screeplot from the R console.

A screeplot displays the eigenvalues associated with a component in descending order versus the number of the component or factor. You can use screeplots in principal components analysis to visually assess which components or factors explain most of the variability in the data, that is it helps us to determine how many components should be retained:

```
# Plot the eigenvalues
barplot(res$eig[, 2], names.arg=1:nrow(res$eig),
        main = "Variances by Component",
        xlab = "Principal Components",
        ylab = "% of variances",
        col ="steelblue")
```

```
# Add connected line segments to the plot
lines(x = 1:nrow(res$eig), res$eig[, 2],
      type="b", pch=19, col = "red")
```

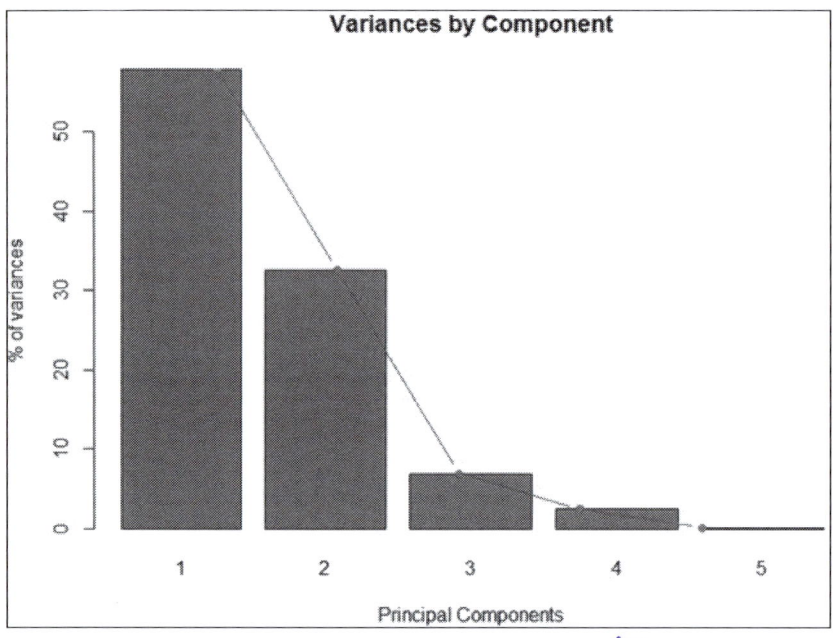

One category of information to which we must pay attention is Cos2 as it helps us to determine the quality of representation of variables in the map of factors. For example, if we want to know that so well it is represented each of the variables for the first two principal components, we could do the following in the R console:

```
# Getting Cos2 or quality of variables on the factor map
cos2<-res$var$cos2[,1:2]
Total<-apply(cos2, 1, sum)
cos2<-cbind(cos2,Total)
x<- c("Comp.1","Comp.2","Total")
cos2<- as.data.frame(round(cos2*100,2))
colnames(cos2) <- c("Comp.1","Comp.2","Total")

cos2
        Comp.1 Comp.2 Total
Maths    80.25  11.92 92.16
Science  52.24  42.04 94.29
English  37.32  51.45 88.77
History  35.99  56.02 92.01
Sports   83.53   1.43 84.96
```

When, in the preceding table, `cos2` of a variable is close to 100, its representation on the map of factors is excellent, and the cutoff must be defined depending on the degree of tolerance of the person making the analysis, by reference, above 60 is a good value.

Continuing the example, other information that we can generate from our PCA model is the contribution of each variable:

```
# Variable contributions
round(res$var$contrib,2)
         Dim.1 Dim.2 Dim.3 Dim.4 Dim.5
Maths    27.74  7.32 19.20  6.82 38.92
Science  18.06 25.81  0.16 45.38 10.59
English  12.90 31.59 31.62  0.49 23.40
History  12.44 34.40 15.54 19.95 17.68
Sports   28.87  0.88 33.48 27.36  9.41
```

 A variable's contributions in the determination of a given principal component are: *(var.cos2 * 100) / (total cos2 of the component)*

We previously verified the quality of the representation of the variables, it is possible to check the quality of representation of individuals with `Cos2`. In fact, this is very important because individuals who are poorly represented may be excluded from the graphical analysis:

```
# Getting Cos2 or quality of individuals on the factor map
cos2<-res$ind$cos2[,1:2]
Total<-apply(cos2, 1, sum)
cos2<-cbind(cos2,Total)
x<- c("Comp.1","Comp.2","Total")
cos2<- as.data.frame(round(cos2*100,2))
colnames(cos2) <- c("Comp.1","Comp.2","Total")

cos2
          Comp.1 Comp.2 Total
Rosa        2.23  67.04 69.27
Denis      13.99  84.84 98.83
Edgar      51.45  13.61 65.06
Yeison     93.69   0.64 94.33
Silvia      8.41  65.64 74.05
Arturo     73.27  26.20 99.47
Elizabeth   0.19  88.61 88.80
Erik       67.36  27.09 94.45
Dante      80.88  13.76 94.65
Sasha      30.86  67.79 98.64
```

In our example, Arturo is represented in 99.47% within the map of factors, while Edgar gets the lowest level of representation with 65.06%. As the purpose of this example, we are working with a minimum level of representation of 60. It is not necessary to exclude individuals from analysis.

The same way as with variables, it is possible to know the level of contribution of each individual to each principal component:

```
#   Contributions of Individuals
round(res$ind$contrib,2)
            Dim.1 Dim.2 Dim.3 Dim.4 Dim.5
Rosa         0.36 19.29 41.46  0.25  0.01
Denis        1.53 16.49  0.61  0.04 17.12
Edgar        3.47  1.63 11.41 21.75 22.96
Yeison      34.78  0.42  4.21 37.47  4.39
Silvia       0.83 11.45 20.13  1.98 17.12
Arturo      10.09  6.41  0.47  0.36  0.72
Elizabeth    0.02 13.13  7.39  1.13  0.19
Erik        13.99  9.99  8.48  3.19  0.34
Dante       31.98  9.67  5.81 33.41  1.61
Sasha        2.95 11.51  0.02  0.42 35.53
```

Additional visual support for PCA

We have seen how it is possible to generate `biplot` graphics. However, this type of graphics has serious limitations when the number of observations increases, and they become very confusing and difficult to interpret.

We will now see an alternative, the factor maps for PCA models:

```
#Loading or installing package FactoMineR
suppressWarnings(
        suppressMessages(if
                        (!require(FactoMineR, quietly=TRUE))
                install.packages("FactoMineR")))
library(FactoMineR)

# Load dataset students
path<-"file:///C:/Unsupervised Learning/Students.csv" # Set your
Path Here
Students <- read.table(path, header=TRUE,
  sep=";", na.strings="NA", dec=",", row.names=1,
strip.white=TRUE)
```

```
Students.PCA<-Students[, c("Maths", "Science", "English",
"History",
  "Sports")]

# Build the PCA in FactoMiner
res<-PCA(Students.PCA , scale.unit=TRUE, ncp=5, graph = FALSE)

# Plot for variables

plot.PCA(res, axes=c(1, 2), choix="var", new.plot=TRUE,
col.var="#ff0000",
  col.quanti.sup="blue", label=c("var", "quanti.sup"),
lim.cos2.var=0,
  title="Variables Factor Map")
```

This code builds a map of factors for the variables of our PCA from students, and contains a circle of correlations in which all variables are represented:

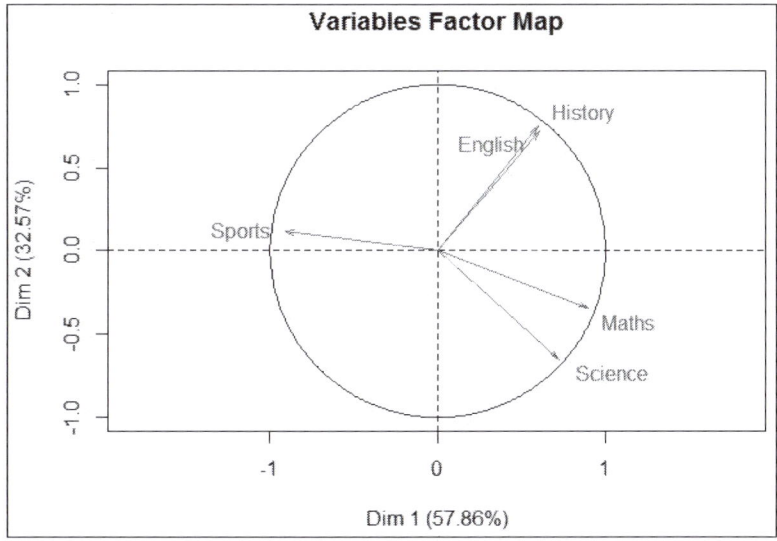

The correlation circle has a scale from -1 to 1 and is useful to compare the first two principal components in relation to variables. The variance explained by these components, that is the level at which the graph represents the reality of the entire dataset, is the sum of the percentages in the diagram: 57.86% + 32.57%. This means that the chart reflects 90.43% of the variance in the data.

In the circle of correlations, each variable is displayed as an arrow (the angles between these arrows indicate the level of correlation between them) For example, if in comparing the two variables, the angle between them is very small, as is the case with English and History, which implies that there is a positive correlation, that is, the marks obtained by students in these subjects behave similarly and vary in the same direction.

Furthermore, while comparing two variables, if the angle is too large such as in the case of math and sports, it implies that there is a negative correlation. That is, increasing performance in math, the performance in sports tends to decrease.

The circle of correlations also provides information on the quality of the representation of variables. Considering that correlation behaves similar to the cosine, the variables best represented will be those with correlations close to 1 and -1, which is, whose arrows approach the border of the circle.

Individuals can also be represented graphically, `FactoMineR` allows us to build a map of factors, such as the following:

```
# Plot for individuals
plot.PCA(res, axes=c(1, 2), choix="ind", habillage="none",
  col.ind="#0000ff", col.ind.sup="blue", col.quali="magenta",
label=c("ind","ind.sup", "quali"),new.plot=TRUE, title=" Individuals
Factor Map")
```

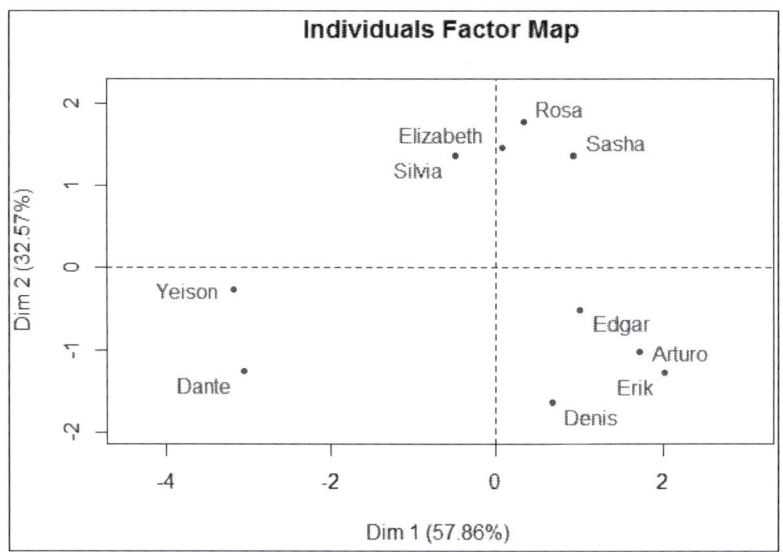

All individuals are represented on the map of factors. It should be emphasized that it is recommended to not represent individuals whose square cosines indicates that they will not be properly represented in the plane of the components chosen. Similar individuals tend to form clusters on the map of factors.

Even though we analyzed the two possible graphical outputs of PCA, an intuitive but interesting trick is to overlap the two charts:

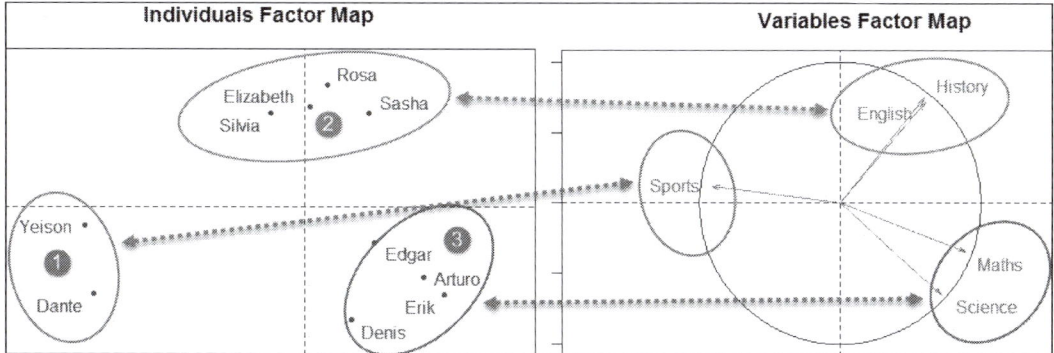

As shown in the preceding chart, to the left, three groups of individuals are visually detected. These groups of individuals may be related to variable groups to the right and you can analyze them together:

Group number 1, consisting of individuals *Yeison* and *Dante* is impacted positively by the results in sports. That is, these individuals are good athletes. Noting the correlation of variables, we can say that they are not as good in science and math as they are inversely correlated variables.

Group number 2, consisting of individuals *Silvia*, *Elizabeth*, *Rosa*, and *Sasha*, groups individuals with good performance in English and History, though they are not great at sports but, at least, they are not the worst because they are located on the axis dividing the quadrants.

Finally, group number 3, consisting of individuals *Edgar*, *Arturo*, *Erik*, and *Denis*, behaves in a manner contrary to group 1 because it contains individuals who are good at science and math, but not at sports.

Advanced tools for plotting PCA

We have explained two types of graphs for analysis of main components: the biplots and maps of individual factors and variables. There is a specialized package called *factoextra* that allows us to enhance the maps of factors and individuals:

factoextra provides some easy-to-use functions to extract and visualize the output of **Principal Component Analysis (PCA)**, **Correspondence Analysis (CA)**, and **Multiple Correspondence Analysis (MCA)**.

As a first step, we must install the package. This time, the installation is a little different because *factoextra* is not published in the CRAN and we must install it from a project site in GitHub (`https://github.com/kassambara/factoextra`). In order to do this, we need to install an additional package called *devtools*, which contains utilities for package development in R, we must also have previously installed *FactoMiner*:

```
#Loading or installing packages
suppressWarnings(
        suppressMessages(if
                        (!require(devtools, quietly=TRUE))
                install.packages("devtools")))
suppressWarnings(
        suppressMessages(if
                        (!require(stringi, quietly=TRUE))
                install.packages("stringi")))
suppressWarnings(
        suppressMessages(if
                        (!require(Rcpp, quietly=TRUE))
                install.packages("Rcpp")))
#Loading or installing package "factoextra"

library("devtools")
install_github("kassambara/factoextra")
```

 Since it is an external resource to CRAN, the installation of `factoextra` might give you some problems. After installing devtools using the instruction: `install_github` (Kassambara / factoextra) , whether or not the console indicates that R cannot find a particular package, it is necessary to install it and run the installation instructions again, as many times as necessary.

Once the required packages are installed, we can make some enhanced graphics through the functions included in *factoextra*. For example, it is much easier to generate a screeplot. Its graphic quality is higher and requires less code:

```
library(factoextra)
# Visualize eigenvalues/variances
fviz_screeplot(res,addlabels=TRUE)
```

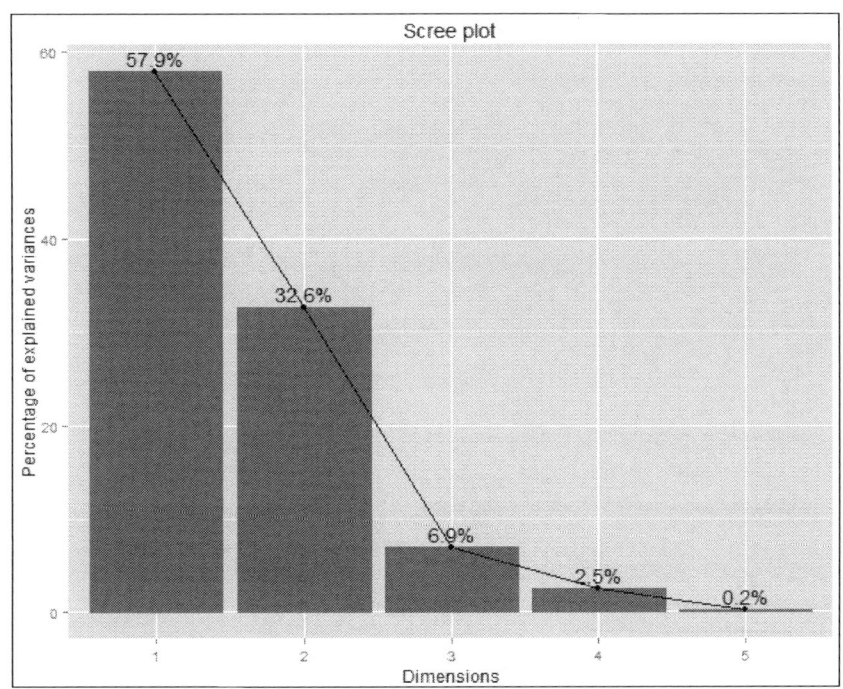

It is also possible to plot the circle of correlations, adding interesting features for analysis. For example, consider a circle of correlation for which we use a gradient color to indicate the level of contribution of each variable:

```
# Control variable colors using their contributions
# Use gradient color
library(ggplot2)
p<-fviz_pca_var(res, col.var="contrib")
```

```
suppressWarnings(p+scale_color_gradient2
                (low="red",high="blue",midpoint = 90)
                +theme_minimal())
```

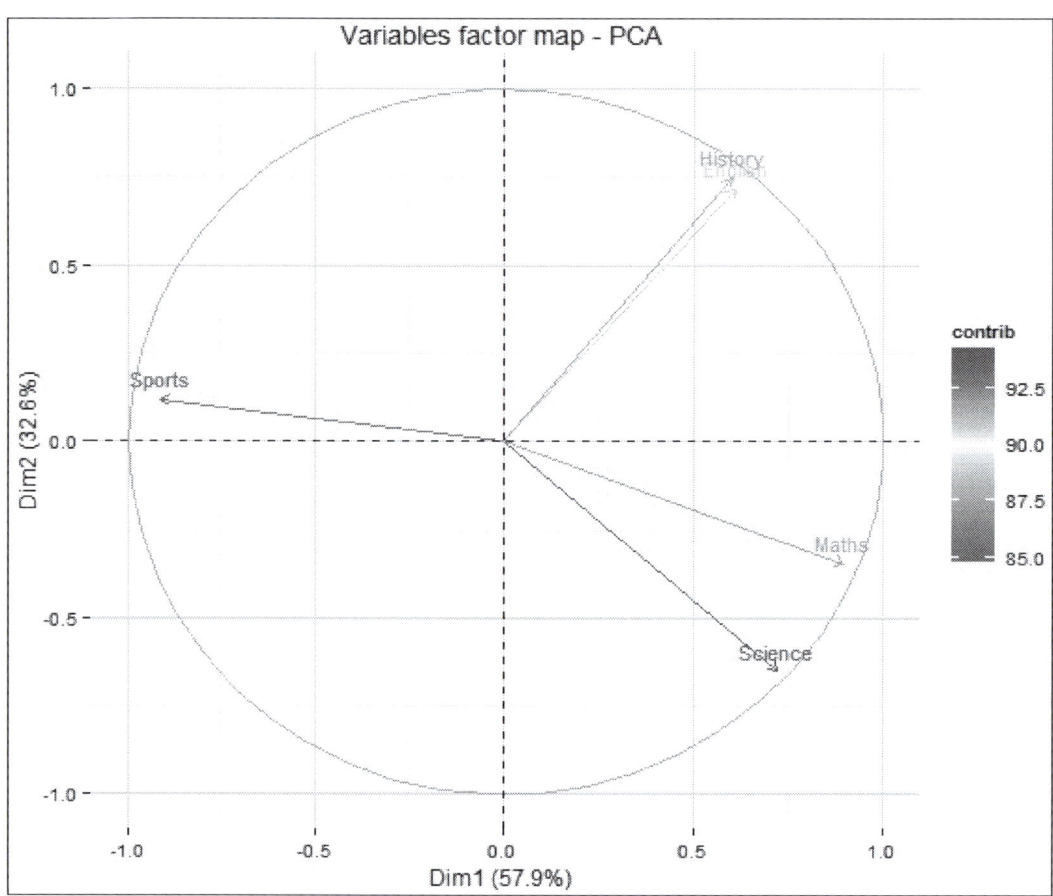

An important aspect of the `factoextra` package is considering that it uses the library `ggplot2` to add great graphic possibilities. The package inherited one of the problems in `ggplot2`, and it is not easy to create multiplots.

This is an important feature in many occasions; however, to resolve this, you can use a costumed function.

In the following example, we will plot the contributions of variables and individuals to the first two principal components using a 2x1 multiplot using factoextra:

```
# Multiple plot function
multiplot <- function(..., plotlist=NULL, file, cols=1,
layout=NULL) {
  library(grid)
  # Make a list from the ... arguments and plotlist
  plots <- c(list(...), plotlist)
  numPlots = length(plots)
  # If layout is NULL, then use 'cols' to determine layout
  if (is.null(layout)) {
    # Make the panel
    # ncol: Number of columns of plots
    # nrow: Number of rows needed, calculated from # of cols
    layout <- matrix(seq(1, cols * ceiling(numPlots/cols)),
                 ncol = cols, nrow = ceiling(numPlots/cols))}
  if (numPlots==1) {
    print(plots[[1]]) }

else {# Set up the page
    grid.newpage()
    pushViewport(viewport(layout = grid.layout(nrow(layout),
ncol(layout))))

    # Make each plot, in the correct location
    for (i in 1:numPlots) {
      # Get the i,j matrix positions of the regions that contain this
subplot
      matchidx <- as.data.frame(which(layout == i, arr.ind = TRUE))

      print(plots[[i]], vp = viewport(layout.pos.row = matchidx$row,
                                  layout.pos.col = matchidx$col))
    } } }

# Variable contributions on axes 1 + 2
p1<-fviz_contrib(res, choice="var", axes = 1:2)
```

```
# Individuals contributions on axes 1 + 2
p2<-fviz_contrib(res, choice="ind", axes = 1:2)

multiplot(p1, p2,cols=2)
```

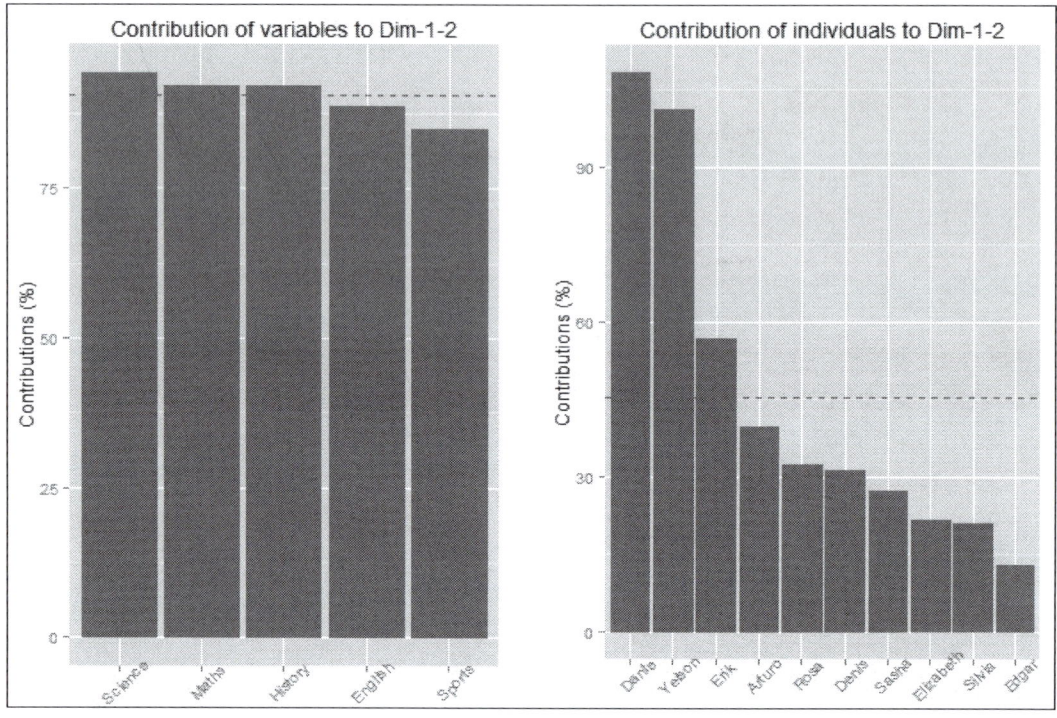

As can be seen, both graphs are presented in the same row, next to each other. If you do not use the custom function, the R console will graph individually.

To conclude this section, we will see a final example. To develop it, we will quickly build a PCA on the Iris dataset (we have already worked with this data in previous chapters). The reason for this is that we will need more data so that the example can be appreciated correctly:

```
data(iris)
resIris <- prcomp(iris[, -5],  scale = TRUE)
# Add Color by groups
p <- fviz_pca_ind(resIris, geom = "point",
    habillage=iris$Species, addEllipses=TRUE,
    ellipse.level= 0.90)+ theme_minimal()
p
```

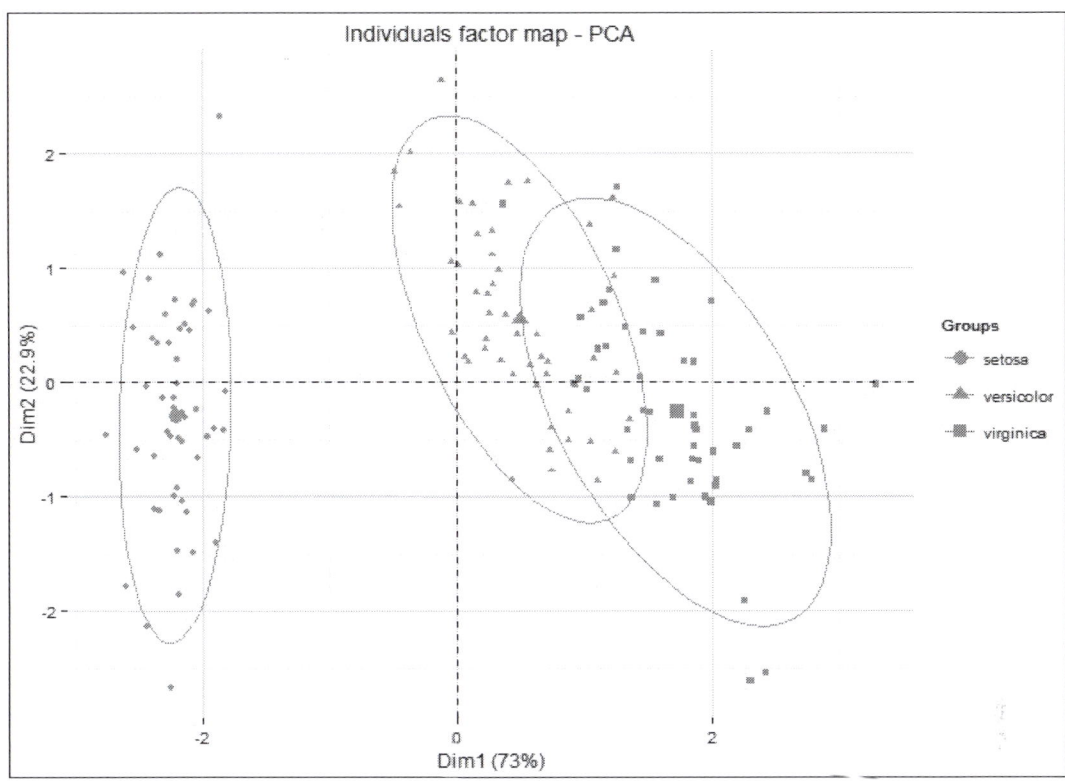

The interesting thing about this chart is that it provides similar functionality to the circle of correlation, with the advantage that it is possible to identify the class of individuals by ellipses, in this case representing the type of plant.

Hierarchical clustering on principal components

Now that we've seen some generalities with respect to principal component analysis, we will combine this knowledge with what we developed in *Chapter 3, Identifying and Understanding Groups: Clustering Algorithms*, when we learned to build agglomerative hierarchical clustering on the original variables of the Iris dataset. In this section we will do it using synthetic variables that we built by principal components analysis.

For this example, we will again use the Iris dataset to build a principal component analysis and then, we will carry out a hierarchical clustering on the principal components, using the **HCPC** function, which is a part of the package FactoMiner.

In the words of its author:

> *"HCPC: Hierarchical Clustering on Principle Components performs an agglomerative hierarchical clustering on results from a factor analysis. Results include paragons, description of the clusters, and graphics."*

```
# Load data from Iris.csv

directory<-c("C:/Unsupervised Learning/Chapter 03/iris.csv")
Iris <- read.table(directory,header=TRUE, sep=",",
                   na.strings="NA", dec=".", strip.white=TRUE)


# Load FactoMiner

suppressWarnings(
        suppressMessages(if
                            (!require(FactoMineR, quietly=TRUE))
                 install.packages("FactoMineR")))

# Build the PCA
Iris.PCA<-Iris[, c("X", "Sepal.Length", "Sepal.Width",
"Petal.Length","Petal.Width")]
 res<-PCA(Iris.PCA , scale.unit=TRUE, ncp=5, graph = FALSE)

# Build the Hierarchical Clustering
 suppressWarnings(res.hcpc<-HCPC(res ,nb.clust=-1,
                          consol=TRUE,min=1,max=3,graph=FALSE))
```

At this point, the clustering on the principal components has already been done. We can check the number of observations in each cluster that has been defined:

```
# Check the clusters size
 table(res.hcpc$data.clust[,ncol(res.hcpc$data.clust),drop=F])


 1   2   3
50  53  47
```

In addition, the function can generate several graphs related to hierarchical clustering models that we built:

```
par(mfrow = c(1, 2))
  # plots a factor map, individuals colored by cluster
 plot.HCPC(res.hcpc, choice="map",draw.tree=FALSE)
 # Build plots of inertia gains.
 plot.HCPC(res.hcpc, choice="bar")
```

In the chart below, to the left we can see the map of factors for individuals. We can identify three clusters by color. On the right, we find a bar chart summarizing the Inter-Cluster inertia gains that can be used as support to know where to prune the dendrogram, that is, how many groups use:

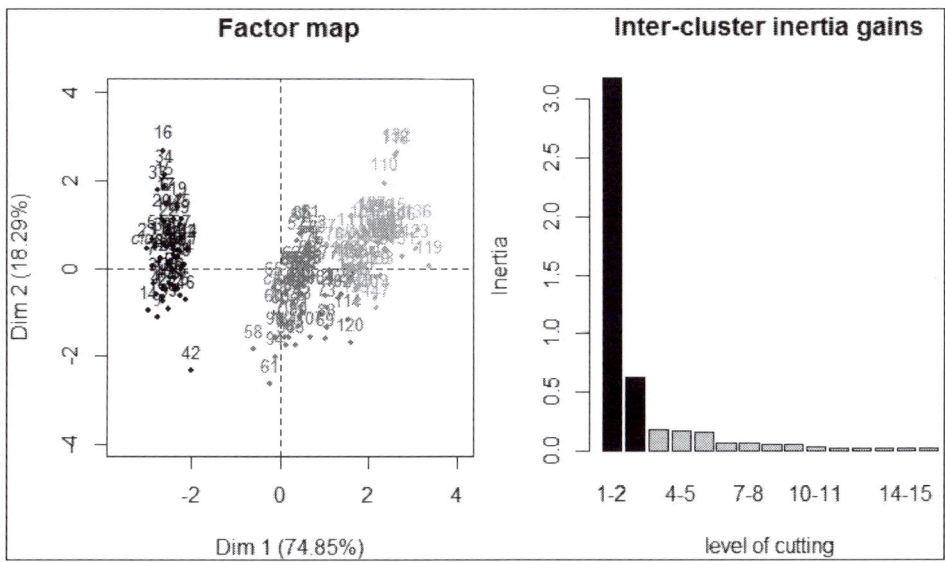

We can also generate the dendrogram, bottom-left, and an interesting plot that mixes a map of factors with a tree in which you can find the clusters identified as follows:

```
   par(mfrow = c(1, 2))
  # Plots the tree
 plot.HCPC(res.hcpc, choice="tree",rect=TRUE,
         tree.barplot=FALSE,t.level="all")
 # Plots the same factor map, individuals colored by cluster, the tree
above
```

```
plot.HCPC(res.hcpc, choice="3D.map",
          angle=60,ind.names=FALSE,centers.plot=TRUE)
```

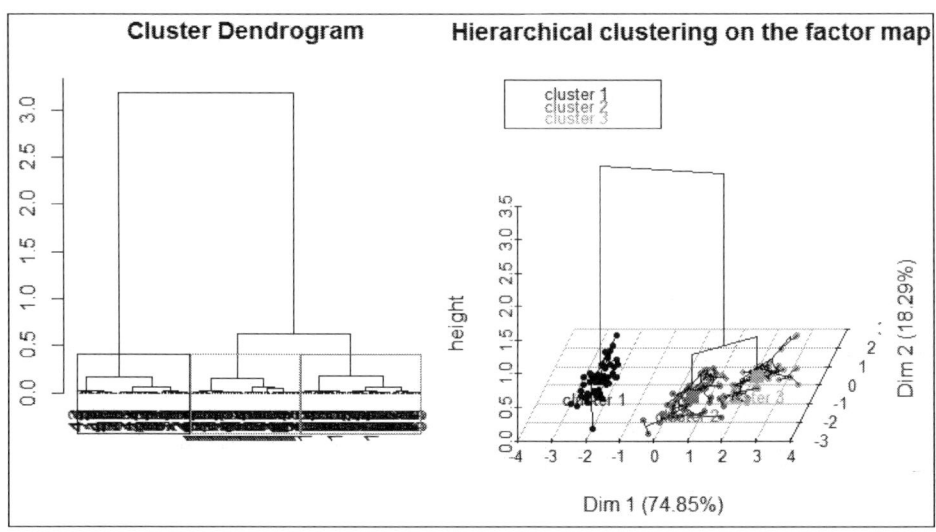

Principal components analysis by user interfaces

Sometimes it is useful to use end-user tools, either because we don't have programming knowledge to R, or simply because they save time. The `FactoMiner` package has a version integrated with the end user tool *Rcommander*:

Rcommander or *Rcmdr* is a visual user interface for working with R, using input commands. It is a very good alternative to start learning R without the need to write programming code directly.

The `Rcmdr` package is a standard R package, and it installs and is loaded in the normal manner:

```
# Install Rcmd
install.packages("Rcmdr")
```

The original installation of `Rcmdr` does not include `FactoMiner`. We need to install it later using the following statement:

```
# Install FactoMiner GUI

source("http://factominer.free.fr/install-facto.r")
```

Depending on the operating system that we use, the installation of Factominer and *Rcmmdr* may be different, or it could give rise to some problems. If you experience any complications, you will find more information on their official websites: http://factominer. free.fr/ and http://www.rcommander.com/.

To load the Rcmdr package once it is installed, simply enter the following command:

```
#Set language to English
 Sys.setenv(LANGUAGE="en")
#Load Rcmdr
 library(Rcmdr)
```

The preceding statement loads the user interface Rcomdr, which should already be integrated with the plugin FactoMiner. The first thing to do is load the data using the menu: Factominer "Import data from textfile"

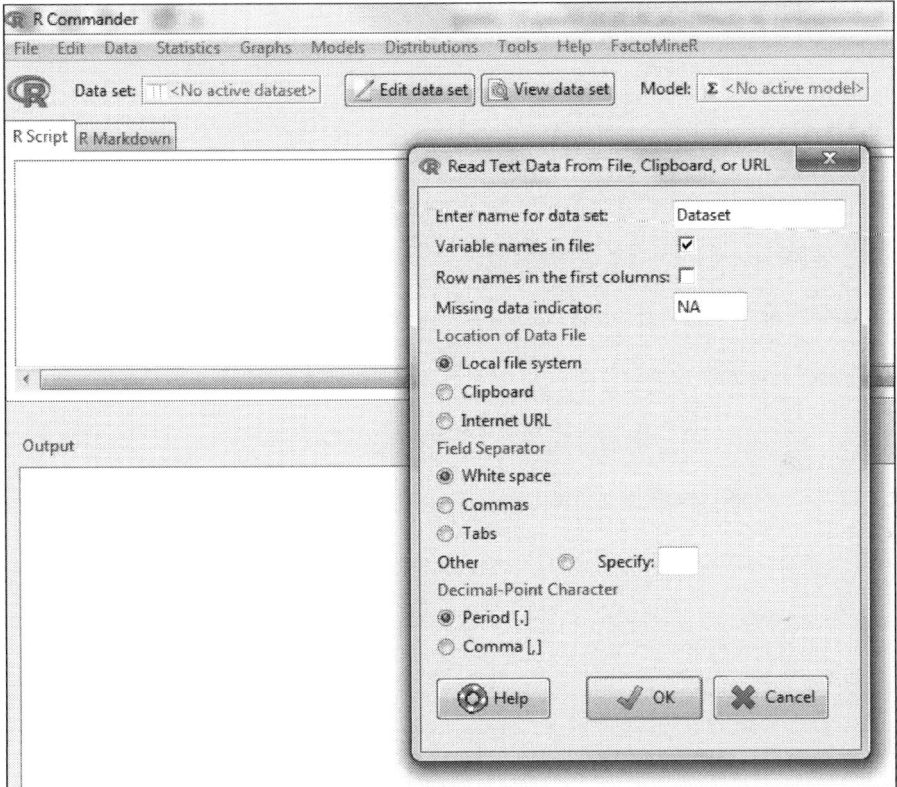

Once the data is loaded, the options for the analysis of principal components and other things is enabled. Using the menu: FactoMiner: Principal Components Analysis, we can even request to conduct a clustering on the PCA:

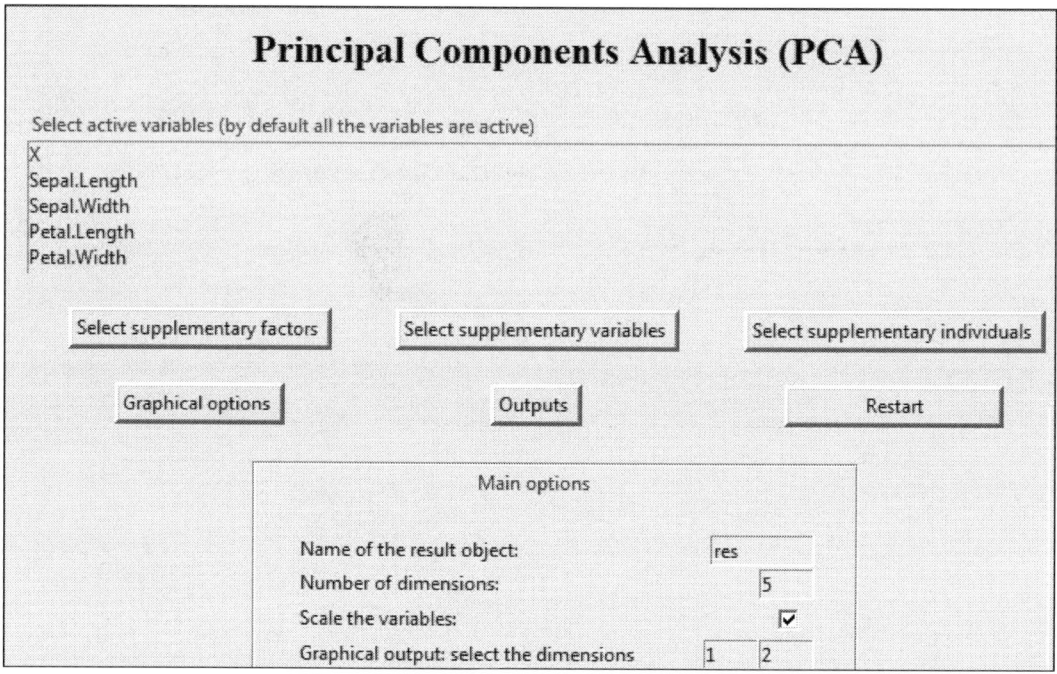

If we talk about tools for end-user interfaces, in addition to integration of the tools that we have seen, it is very interesting to know the FactoShiny package:

FactoShiny performs factorial analysis with a menu and draws graphs interactively; thanks to FactoMiner and a Shiny application. This package minimizes interaction with the console. We must load the data to the R environment as we have seen. Then it is only necessary to use a function that will receive the loaded data as parameter. For example:

```
#Load data in a data.frame named Iris
suppressWarnings(
        suppressMessages(if
                        (!require(Factoshiny, quietly=TRUE))
                install.packages("Factoshiny")))
```

```
#Load data in a data.frame named Iris
directory<-c("C:/Unsupervised Learning/Chapter 03/iris.csv")
Iris <- read.table(directory,header=TRUE, sep=",",
                    na.strings="NA", dec=".", strip.white=TRUE)

#Performs Principal Component Analysis (PCA) a Shiny application.
PCAshiny(Iris)
```

After this is done, FactoShiny is displayed on our web browser, in which we interact through menu options. For example, the **Data** menu:

PCA on the Iris dataset

Graphs   Values   Automatic description of axes   Summary of dataset   Data

Show 10 entries   Search:

Names	X	Sepal.Length	Sepal.Width	Petal.Length	Petal.Width	Species
1	1	5.1	3.5	1.4	0.2	setosa
2	2	4.9	3.0	1.4	0.2	setosa
3	3	4.7	3.2	1.3	0.2	setosa
4	4	4.6	3.1	1.5	0.2	setosa
5	5	5.0	3.6	1.4	0.2	setosa
6	6	5.4	3.9	1.7	0.4	setosa
7	7	4.6	3.4	1.4	0.3	setosa
8	8	5.0	3.4	1.5	0.2	setosa
9	9	4.4	2.9	1.4	0.2	setosa
10	10	4.9	3.1	1.5	0.1	setosa
Names	X	Sepal.Length	Sepal.Width	Petal.Length	Petal.Width	Species

We can also use the **Summary of dataset** option for exploratory data analysis:

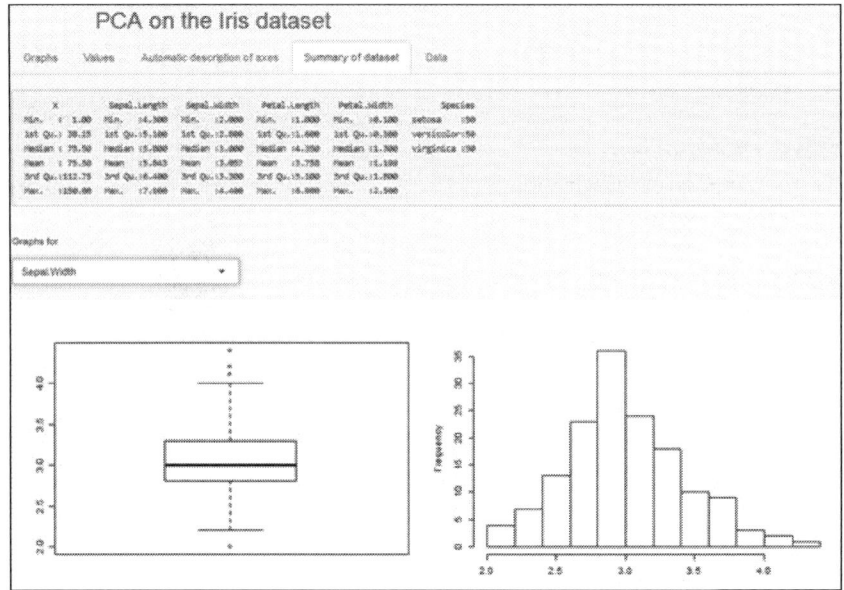

Alternatively, interact with graphs and data obtained from the analysis of main components:

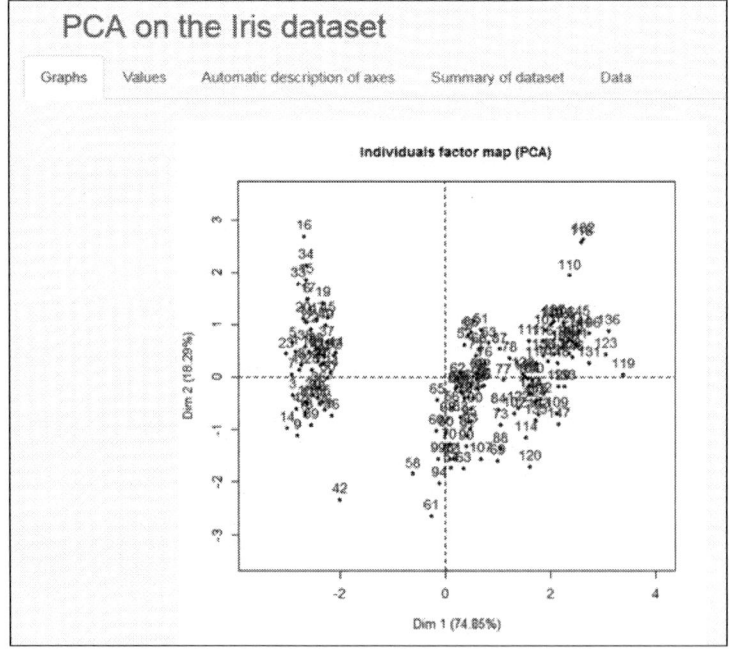

Summary

In this chapter, we began by reviewing the concept of dimensionality reduction. We saw that its importance is mainly in datasets of high dimensionality. The quality of the models tend to worsen due to what's known as the curse of dimensionality, which was explained through an example. Next, we discussed some possibilities to mitigate the negative effects of high dimensionality. This was done by feature selection techniques and feature extraction. We concentrated on the latter by analyzing the most widely used technique, PCA.

As an added value, we detail the use of a specialized package to enhance graphics for PCA analysis. The package `factoextra` exemplifies some extended possibilities for this kind of graphics. Later, we linked what was previously learned in the third chapter with this chapter, by building agglomerative hierarchical clustering on Principal Components Analysis. Finally, we ended the chapter showing some options regarding PCA using end-user interfaces.

In the next chapter, we will see how to combat the curse of dimensionality from another angle, using feature selection techniques that do not affect changes in the data, and will instead apply techniques to discern which variables do not add value in a dataset and the omission of which contributes to modeling of higher quality.

6
Feature Selection Methods

In the previous chapter, we discussed the problems faced while working with high-dimensional datasets, sometimes called **the curse of dimensionality**. In this regard, we commented on how there are two ways to deal with the problem: by methods of dimensionality reduction, and through feature selection methods; in this chapter, we will focus on the latter.

This chapter aims to explain some techniques for feature selection, also known as variable selection or attribute selection. Feature selection is the process of selecting a subset of relevant features for use in model construction.

The key point is to choose a subset of relevant features of variables for modeling and to not use features that prove to be redundant considering their correlation to simplifying model construction.

Most advances and developments in relation to feature selection have been made in the field of supervised learning, for classifiers-based models. By contrast, in the field of unsupervised learning, deciding which variables we will use is a complex issue.

In this chapter, we will be covering the following aspects:

- The concept of feature selection
- The most commonly used techniques:
  - Expert knowledge-based
  - Feature ranking
  - Subset selection techniques
  - Embedded methods
  - Wrapper methods
  - Filter methods

Feature selection techniques

Feature selection techniques do not modify the original representation of the variables, since only a subset out of them is selected. These techniques preserve the original semantics of the variables, offering the advantage of interpretability.

Unsupervised feature selection algorithms assume that no classifiers are available for the dataset. For this reason, the aim changes from identifying features relevant to making a prediction, to finding the features that contribute the most information to the dataset.

We can generalize the benefit of performing feature selection into three major aspects:

- They help us to reduce the effects of the curse of dimensionality, that is, to improve the performance of our models
- They reduce the time and resources required to process our models
- They help models to be easier to interpret

Whatever the benefit that we are seeking, it is possible to use a variety of methods to perform feature selection. For example: expert knowledge-based techniques, feature ranking techniques, and subset selection techniques, as seen in the following hierarchy:

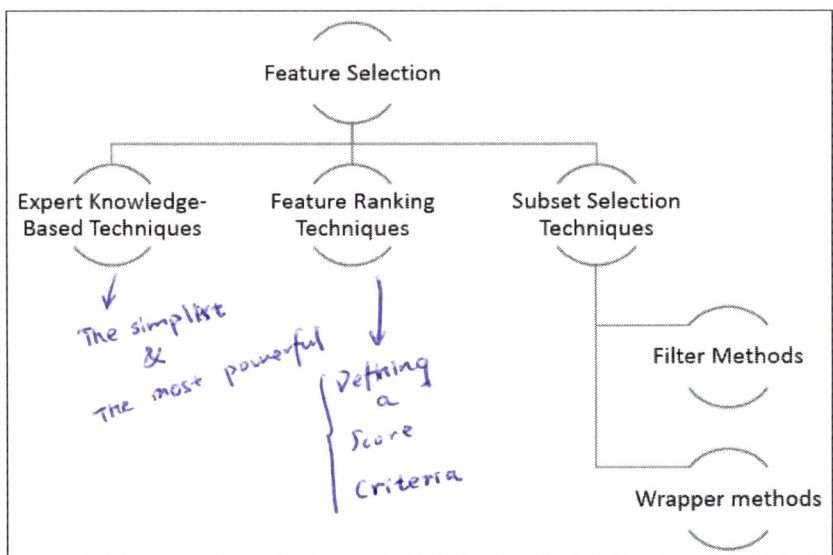

Expert knowledge-based techniques

Beginning with the simplest option, and very often the most powerful, resorting to expert knowledge may be the first approach, that is, a person with enough knowledge of the problem may be the first filter. The reason for this is that there may exist aspects of the problem and the data, which could escape numerical approximations. For example, an expert in the data may suggest excluding certain variables, considering functional aspects that, otherwise, we could not know of.

Feature ranking

Feature ranking is a technique aimed at supporting expert knowledge, and consists of defining a scoring criteria, calculating the performance of each variable individually and listing them in descending order. This method does not determine the cutoff point; the user should define the level from which the variables are excluded.

For example, suppose we have a dataset of 14 variables. The first step is to proceed to define a qualification criterion for each variable. This could be an approach based on correlation, for example the Pearson correlation coefficient. Also, assume that we want to use only the best five variables:

Ranking	Variable Name	Score
01	V07	0,94
02	V14	0,81
03	V04	0,78
04	V05	0,76
05	V03	0,75
06	V11	0,73
07	V01	0,63
08	V02	0,57
09	V10	0,33
10	V13	0,24
11	V08	0,22
12	V06	0,10
13	V12	0,09
14	V09	0,01
Threshold=0.75		

Subsequently, a validation can be performed to compare the performance of clustering with all data versus a model that uses only the data selected by ranking variables.

To apply the concept directly on the R console, the following is a possible example, using the package FSelector.

`FSelector` is a package containing functions for selecting attributes from a given dataset.

Regarding the data for this example, we use the dataset `BostonHousing`.

This is housing data for 506 census tracts of Boston from the 1970 census. The dataframe `BostonHousing` contains the original data by Harrison and Rubinfeld (1979). More details about this dataset can be found in the `mlbench` package.

As usual, the first step is to install and load the packages in the R environment along with the necessary data:

```
#Loading or installing package
suppressWarnings(
        suppressMessages(if
                        (!require(FSelector, quietly=TRUE))
                install.packages("FSelector")))
library(FSelector)


# Loading Data
path<-"file:///C:/Unsupervised Learning/Chapter
06/BostonHousing.csv" # Set your Path Here

Dataset<-read.csv(path, sep = ",", dec = ".",row.names = 1)
Dataset<-Dataset[-4]
str(Dataset)
head(Dataset)
```

```
Console C:/Unsupervised Learning/Chapter 06/
> str(Dataset)
'data.frame':   506 obs. of  13 variables:
 $ crim   : num  0.00632 0.02731 0.02729 0.03237 0.06905 ...
 $ zn     : num  18 0 0 0 0 12.5 12.5 12.5 12.5 ...
 $ indus  : num  2.31 7.07 7.07 2.18 2.18 2.18 7.87 7.87 7.87 7.87 ...
 $ nox    : num  0.538 0.469 0.469 0.458 0.458 0.458 0.524 0.524 0.524 0.524
 $ rm     : num  6.58 6.42 7.18 7 7.15 ...
 $ age    : num  65.2 78.9 61.1 45.8 54.2 58.7 66.6 96.1 100 85.9 ...
 $ dis    : num  4.09 4.97 4.97 6.06 6.06 ...
 $ rad    : num  1 2 2 3 3 3 5 5 5 5 ...
 $ tax    : num  296 242 242 222 222 222 311 311 311 311 ...
 $ ptratio: num  15.3 17.8 17.8 18.7 18.7 18.7 15.2 15.2 15.2 15.2 ...
 $ b      : num  397 397 393 395 397 ...
 $ lstat  : num  4.98 9.14 4.03 2.94 5.33 ...
 $ medv   : num  24 21.6 34.7 33.4 36.2 28.7 22.9 27.1 16.5 18.9 ...
> head(Dataset)
     crim zn indus   nox    rm  age    dis rad tax ptratio      b lstat medv
1 0.00632 18  2.31 0.538 6.575 65.2 4.0900   1 296    15.3 396.90  4.98 24.0
2 0.02731  0  7.07 0.469 6.421 78.9 4.9671   2 242    17.8 396.90  9.14 21.6
3 0.02729  0  7.07 0.469 7.185 61.1 4.9671   2 242    17.8 392.83  4.03 34.7
4 0.03237  0  2.18 0.458 6.998 45.8 6.0622   3 222    18.7 394.63  2.94 33.4
5 0.06905  0  2.18 0.458 7.147 54.2 6.0622   3 222    18.7 396.90  5.33 36.2
6 0.02985  0  2.18 0.458 6.430 58.7 6.0622   3 222    18.7 394.12  5.21 28.7
```

The data is successfully loaded and contains 13 numeric variables.

The `FSelector` package contains a variety of different algorithms to rank the variables. Continuing with the example, we will use the correlation coefficient as a unit of valuation:

```
# Making the scores
Scores <- linear.correlation(medv~., Dataset)
Scores
        attr_importance
crim         0.3883046
zn           0.3604453
indus        0.4837252
nox          0.4273208
rm           0.6953599
age          0.3769546
dis          0.2499287
rad          0.3816262
tax          0.4685359
ptratio      0.5077867
b            0.3334608
lstat        0.7376627
```

In the previous table, we can observe a list that contains one row for each of the variables on the left and the score on the right. This is the ranking table and, in order to make the decision, we need to define the cutoff. For the purposes of this example, suppose we want to use the top 5 most representative variables. We could do this visually because there are few variables, but in a higher dimensional dataset, it is helpful to use the `cutoff.k` function included in the `FSelector` package:

```
# cutoff.k: The algorithms select a subset from a ranked
# attributes.
# Choosing Variables by cutoff
Subset <- cutoff.k(Scores, 5)
as.data.frame(Subset)
[1] "lstat"   "rm"      "ptratio" "indus"   "tax"
```

The variables that we should choose, according to the rule that we define for this example, are: `"lstat"`, `"rm"`, `"ptratio"`, `"indus"`, and `"tax"`.

We could also set the cutoff as a percentage. Let's see how to indicate that we want to work with 40% of the best variables, which logically comes to the same conclusion:

```
Subset2 <-cutoff.k.percent(Scores, 0.4)
as.data.frame(Subset2)
[1] "lstat"   "rm"       "ptratio" "indus"    "tax"
```

We observe what happens if, instead of making the score for the correlation coefficient, we used an entropy-based approach. The information gain will be as follows:

```
# Making the scores
Scores2 <- information.gain(medv~., Dataset)

# Choosing Variables by cutoffSubset <- cutoff.k(Scores2, 5)
Subset3 <- cutoff.k(Scores2, 5)
as.data.frame(Subset3)

[1] "lstat"   "rm"       "nox"      "indus"    "ptratio"
```

Using the new approach, we reached a similar but not identical result. There are four variables that persist, however one is replaced when using the new scoring method. The selection of the scoring method greatly affects the result. It is recommended to study and test various algorithms to determine which fits best.

Subset selection techniques

In contrast to ranking methods, which only classify the variables individually according to the criteria chosen by the user, subset selection techniques can automatically determine the size of the feature subset.

These techniques typically use a quality measure of variables, in conjunction with a heuristic search method, which aims to find the smallest possible subset of variables without causing a reduction in performance. It can be subdivided into wrapper methods, filter methods, and embedded methods.

Embedded methods

Often, models already have capabilities for feature selection. An embedded method of feature selection is one where the feature selection is native to the model. An example of such solutions is the ewkm function, which is a part of the wskm package.

In the words of its author:

> "ewkm *is an entropy weighted k-means which means that it is a weighted subspace clustering algorithm that is well suited to high dimensional data. Weights are calculated as the importance of a variable with regard to cluster membership.*"

In the following code, we develop a simple use example in the R console. We use the Iris dataset, for the purposes of its comparison with the traditional k-means model, as discussed in *Chapter 3, Identifying and Understanding Groups – Clustering Algorithms*:

```
#Loading or installing package
suppressWarnings(
        suppressMessages(if
                             (!require(wskm, quietly=TRUE))
                install.packages("wskm")))
library(wskm)
set.seed(2)
model <- ewkm(iris[1:4], 3, lambda=2, maxiter=1000)


# Load or install packages
suppressWarnings(
        suppressMessages(if
                             (!require(cluster, quietly=TRUE))
                install.packages("cluster")))
library("cluster")
# Cluster Plot against 1st 2 principal components
clusplot(iris[1:4], model$cluster, color=TRUE, shade=TRUE,
         labels=2, lines=1,main='Cluster Analysis for Iris')
```

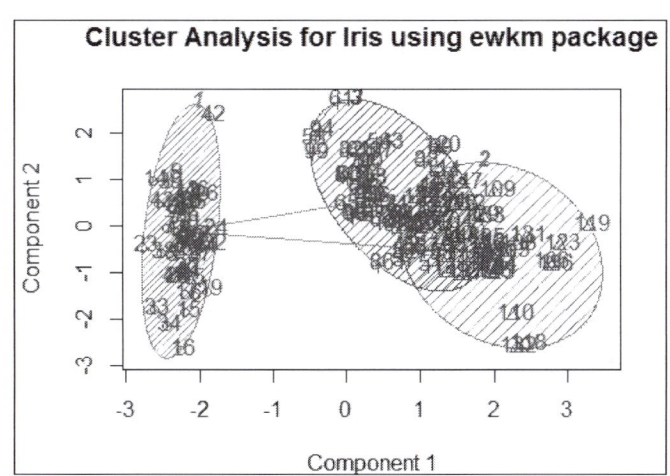

Weights are calculated for each variable and cluster. They are a measure of the relative importance of each variable with regards to the membership of the observations to that cluster. The weights are incorporated into the distance function, typically reducing the distance for more important variables.

Weights remain stored in the model and we can check them as follows:

```
# Show the stored weights
round(model$weights*100,2)
  Sepal.Length Sepal.Width Petal.Length Petal.Width
1         3.62        2.25        36.28       57.86
2         0.07       31.77         0.21       67.96
3         0.10       16.78         0.10       83.02
```

Wrapper methods

Such methods are based on selecting a subset of features and using heuristic search algorithms. One of the major disadvantages of these methods is that in datasets with many variables, they require significant processing time due to their complexity.

These methods are generally associated with supervised learning, but it is possible to use them in unsupervised learning too. For example, in clustering, the inclusion of noise variables can degrade the final model.

In the following diagram, we can observe a wrapper approach for unsupervised learning:

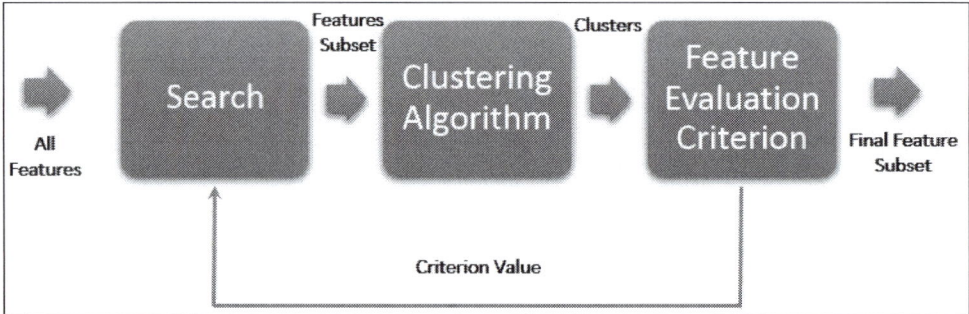

The package `clustvarsel` contains an implementation of such methods to model-based clustering.

In the words of its author:

> "clustvarsel *is a function which implements variable selection methodology for model-based clustering and allows to find the (locally) optimal subset of variables in a dataset that has the group/cluster information. A greedy or headlong search can be used, either in a forward-backward or backward-forward direction, with or without sub-sampling at the hierarchical clustering stage for starting Mclust models.*"

For the following example, we use a synthetic dataset, consisting of five variables, where deliberately only the first two have utility for clustering analysis. The others should be excluded by the method:

```
#Loading data from csv file
path<-"file:///C:/Unsupervised Learning/Chapter
06/syntheticdata.csv" # Set your Path Here
Dataset<-read.csv(path, sep = ",", dec = ".",row.names = 1)
head(Dataset)
          X1          X2          X3          X4        X5
1 -0.71807482 -0.1137642 -1.02888833  0.45394435 1.725742
2  3.75019220  3.3638854  3.43319075 -2.12665936 2.469371
3 -0.44627119 -0.6971258  2.25009635  4.21566323 1.063453
4  0.08522441  0.1547583  0.09926313  0.07124757 1.691745
5  4.36181004  2.0209057  4.06428491  0.41207853 1.462167
6 -0.52709715  1.2428107 -0.75457360  0.99417826 2.209369
```

After loading the dataset, we proceed to load the required packages and generate an estimation of the optimal subset of variables using clustvarsel, applying the *greedy sequential forward search* algorithm:

```
suppressWarnings(
        suppressMessages(if
                        (!require(clustvarsel, quietly=TRUE))
                install.packages("clustvarsel")))
library(clustvarsel)
suppressWarnings(
        suppressMessages(if
                        (!require(mclust, quietly=TRUE))
                install.packages("mclust")))
library(mclust)
```

```
# sequential forward greedy search (default)
out = clustvarsel(Dataset, G = 1:5)
out
```

```
Console ~/
> out
'clustvarsel' model object:

Stepwise (forward) greedy search:
   variable proposed        BIC  BIC difference  Type of step  Decision
1            X1     -808.2342       19.48093             Add   Accepted
2            X2    -1501.8329       45.82165             Add   Accepted
3            X5    -1501.8329      -11.05185             Add   Rejected
4            X2    -1501.8329       45.82078          Remove   Rejected

Selected subset: X1, X2
>
```

The selection algorithm indicates that the subset we use for the clustering model is composed of variables X1 and X2 and that other variables should be rejected. Having identified the variables that we use, we proceed to build the clustering model:

```
# Clustering produced by the selected variables
Subset1 = Dataset[,out$subset]
mod = Mclust(Subset1, G = 1:5)
summary(mod)
--------------------------------------------------
Gaussian finite mixture model fitted by EM algorithm
--------------------------------------------------
Mclust EEV (ellipsoidal, equal volume and shape) model with 2
components:
 log.likelihood    n    df        BIC         ICL
      -727.074   200    9   -1501.833   -1509.327
Clustering table:
   1     2
 107    93
plot(mod,c("classification"))
```

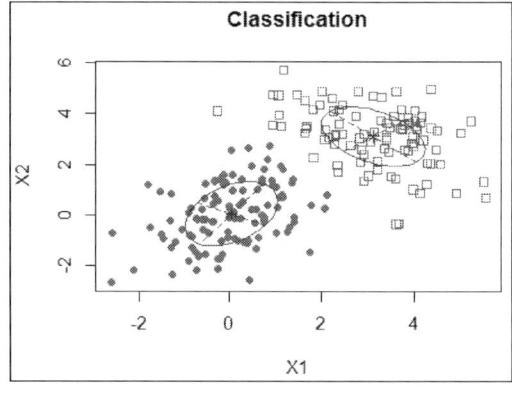

 The package `clustvarsel` has an alternate search method, namely *The headlong search*. Furthermore, an important advantage can be executed by parallel processing in a simple way using the parameter `parallel = TRUE`.

Filter methods

Filter methods evaluate the feature subsets not by running a model on them, but rather by applying some sort of metric. Some types of conventional metrics are:

- **Dependency metrics**: These have the ability to predict one feature from another one. For example, the correlation.

- **Information metrics**: They compare the information gain of individual features. For example, entropy or information gain.

- **Distance metrics**: These aid in the effective separation of the features.

Next is an example of how we can apply a filtering process in R to remove redundancy by correlation, using the dataset `BostonHousing` presented earlier.

We use the `findCorrelation` function included in the `caret` package.

`findCorrelation` is a function that searches through a correlation matrix and returns a vector of integers corresponding to the columns, to remove or reduce pair-wise correlations.

```
# Loading Data

path<-"file:///C:/Unsupervised Learning/Chapter
06/BostonHousing.csv" # Set your Path Here

Dataset<-read.csv(path, sep = ",", dec = ".",row.names = 1)
Dataset<-Dataset[-4]
head(Dataset,3)

#Loading or installing package
suppressWarnings(
        suppressMessages(if
                        (!require(caret, quietly=TRUE))
                install.packages("caret")))
library(caret)
```

```
suppressWarnings(
        suppressMessages(if
                        (!require(corrplot, quietly=TRUE))
                install.packages("corrplot")))
library(corrplot)

# calculate correlation matrix
correlationMatrix <- cor(Dataset)

# find attributes that are highly correlated
highlyCorrelated <- findCorrelation(correlationMatrix,
cutoff=0.75)
# highly correlated attributes
highlyCorrelated
names(Dataset[,highlyCorrelated])


[1] "indus" "tax"    "nox"
```

The variables that have a higher correlation to 0.75 are indus, tax, and nox. We can remove them and compare the results graphically as follows:

```
# Redundant Features Removed
Dataset2<-Dataset[-highlyCorrelated]

#comparing graphically
par(mfrow = c(1, 2))
corrplot(correlationMatrix, order = "hclust")
corrplot(cor(Dataset2), order = "hclust")
```

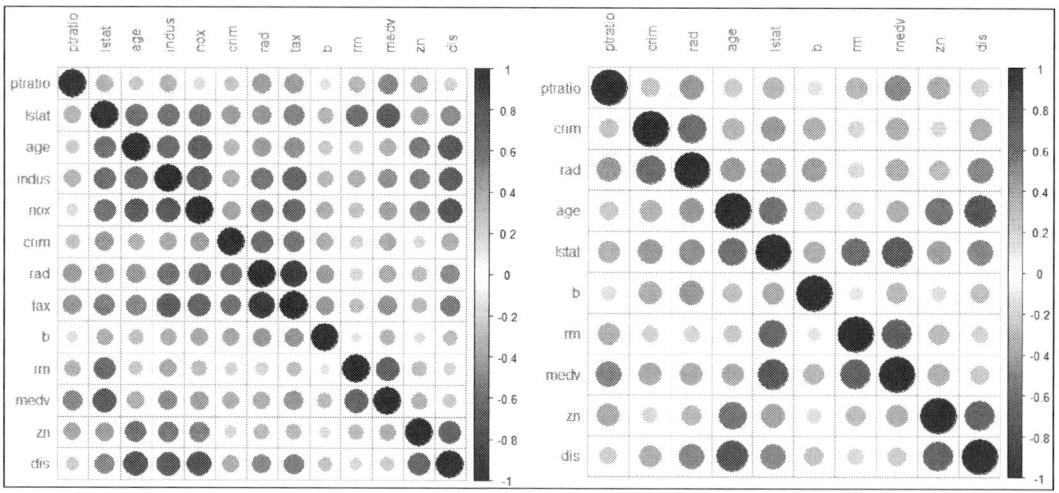

The graph on the left corresponds to the correlation matrix of the original dataset and the graph on the right corresponds to the dataset once we have removed the redundant variables.

Summary

In this chapter, we began by reviewing the concept of feature selection, its importance and the need to include it in unsupervised learning processes. You learned that expert knowledge can be a valuable alternative and that we can enrich it by applying less empirical techniques such as feature ranking or various subset selection techniques.

Dear reader, here ends our little journey through the wide world of unsupervised learning. Thank you very much for your company. I sincerely hope that it was helpful to you. This book is intended to be a modest introduction. We encourage you to go ahead and continue learning so that you can refine and improve what you have learned with us.

References

The author of this book is not the creator of any of the packages, functions, or programs used in each of the examples; I am only a facilitator. For that reason, I would like to sincerely thank the developers of R and the R Packages, who have contributed so generously to the growing of the R open source community. In this book, we use many packages and sometimes the definitions of these packages. In order to be respectful to the authors, they are written verbatim.

This appendix provides a list of links referenced in the book, which are sorted chapter-wise.

Hyperlinks provide a gateway to extensive literature that can be accessed on the Internet. They provide information above and beyond what one finds in a single article, book, blog, or other media formats. However, when one writes a book, the links provided in the printed book are useful to only those readers who would go to any lengths to find information, but for others, these links are irksome, frustrating, and almost useless. They are of course useful in online formats such as e-books.

In order to conform to page-count limits set by the publishers and yet provide guidance to the readers, there is no better way than publishing a list of links that is sorted chapter-wise and placed in a location that is easy to access. This appendix is an attempt to do just that. However, some essential information is used in the book in some chapters.

Chapter 1, Welcome to the Age of Information Technology

About R:

```
https://www.r-project.org/
```

Chapter 2, Working with Data – Exploratory Data Analysis

Iris Dataset: Edgar Anderson's Iris Data:

```
https://stat.ethz.ch/R-manual/R-devel/library/datasets/html/iris.html
```

XLConnect: Excel Connector for R:

```
https://cran.r-project.org/web/packages/XLConnect/index.html
```

Hmisc: Harrell Miscellaneous:

```
https://cran.r-project.org/web/packages/Hmisc/index.html
```

fBasics: Rmetrics - Markets and Basic Statistics:

```
https://cran.r-project.org/web/packages/fBasics/index.html
```

pastecs: Package for Analysis of Space-Time Ecological Series:

```
https://cran.r-project.org/web/packages/pastecs/index.html
```

ggplot2: An Implementation of the Grammar of Graphics:

```
https://cran.r-project.org/web/packages/ggplot2/index.html
```

dplyr: A Grammar of Data Manipulation:

```
https://cran.r-project.org/web/packages/dplyr/index.html
```

gplots: Various R programming tools for plotting data:

```
https://cran.r-project.org/web/packages/gplots/index.html
```

car: Companion to Applied Regression:

```
https://cran.r-project.org/web/packages/car/index.html
```

lattice: Trellis graphics for R:

`https://cran.r-project.org/web/packages/lattice/index.html`

ellipse: Functions for drawing ellipses and ellipse-like confidence regions:

`https://cran.r-project.org/web/packages/ellipse/index.html`

corrplot: Visualization of a correlation matrix:

`https://cran.r-project.org/web/packages/corrplot/index.html`

rattle: Graphical User Interface for Data Mining in R:

`https://cran.r-project.org/web/packages/rattle/index.html`

`http://rattle.togaware.com/`

Chapter 3, Identifying and Understanding Groups – Clustering Algorithms

ElemStatLearn: Data Sets, Functions, and examples from *The Elements of Statistical Learning, Data Mining, Inference, and Prediction* by Trevor Hastie, Robert Tibshirani, and Jerome Friedman:

`https://cran.r-project.org/web/packages/ElemStatLearn/index.html`

`http://statweb.stanford.edu/~tibs/ElemStatLearn/`

reshape: Flexibly reshape data:

`https://cran.r-project.org/web/packages/reshape/index.html`

scatterplot3d: 3D Scatter plot:

`https://cran.r-project.org/web/packages/scatterplot3d/index.html`

NbClust: Determining the Best Number of Clusters in a Data Set:

`https://cran.r-project.org/web/packages/NbClust/index.html`

cluster: "Finding Groups in Data": Cluster Analysis Extended Rousseeuw et al:

`https://cran.r-project.org/web/packages/cluster/index.html`

HSAUR: A Handbook of Statistical Analyses Using R (1st Edition):

`https://cran.r-project.org/web/packages/HSAUR/index.html`

amap: Another Multidimensional Analysis Package:

`https://cran.r-project.org/web/packages/amap/index.html`

cba: Clustering for Business Analytics:

`https://cran.r-project.org/web/packages/cba/index.html`

rattle: Graphical User Interface for Data Mining in R:

`https://cran.r-project.org/web/packages/rattle/index.html`

`http://rattle.togaware.com/`

fpc: Flexible Procedures for Clustering:

`https://cran.r-project.org/web/packages/fpc/index.html`

dendextend: Extending R's Dendrogram Functionality:

`https://cran.r-project.org/web/packages/dendextend/index.html`

corrplot: Visualization of a correlation matrix:

`https://cran.r-project.org/web/packages/corrplot/index.html`

ape: Analyses of Phylogenetics and Evolution:

`https://cran.r-project.org/web/packages/ape/index.html`

Chapter 4, Association Rules

arules: Mining Association Rules and Frequent Itemsets:

`https://cran.r-project.org/web/packages/arules/index.html`

arulesViz: Visualizing Association Rules and Frequent Itemsets:

`https://cran.r-project.org/web/packages/arulesViz/index.html`

Chapter 5, Dimensionality Reduction

SphericalCubature: Numerical integration over spheres and balls in n-dimensions; multivariate polar coordinates:

```
https://cran.r-project.org/web/packages/SphericalCubature/index.html
```

FactoMineR: Multivariate Exploratory Data Analysis and Data Mining:

```
https://cran.r-project.org/web/packages/FactoMineR/index.html
```

```
http://factominer.free.fr/
```

devtools: Tools to Make Developing R Packages Easier:

```
https://cran.r-project.org/web/packages/devtools/index.html
```

stringi: Character String Processing Facilities:

```
https://cran.r-project.org/web/packages/stringi/index.html
```

Rcpp: Seamless R and C++ integration:

```
https://cran.r-project.org/web/packages/Rcpp/index.html
```

factoextra: Visualization of the outputs of a multivariate analysis:

```
https://github.com/kassambara/factoextra
```

Rcmdr: R Commander:

```
https://cran.r-project.org/web/packages/Rcmdr/index.html
```

```
http://www.rcommander.com/
```

Factoshiny: Perform factorial analysis from FactoMineR with a Shiny application:

```
https://cran.r-project.org/web/packages/Factoshiny/index.html
```

Chapter 6, Feature Selection Methods

FSelector: Selecting attributes:

`https://cran.r-project.org/web/packages/FSelector/index.html`

wskm: Weighted k-Means Clustering:

`https://cran.r-project.org/web/packages/wskm/index.html`

cluster: "Finding Groups in Data": Cluster Analysis Extended Rousseeuw et al:

`https://cran.r-project.org/web/packages/cluster/index.html`

clustvarsel: Variable Selection for Model-Based Clustering:

`https://cran.r-project.org/web/packages/clustvarsel/index.html`

mclust: Normal Mixture Modelling for Model-Based Clustering, Classification, and Density Estimation:

`https://cran.fhcrc.org/web/packages/mclust/index.html`

Index

evaluation 10
modeling 10
curse of dimensionality 112-114

D

data
exploring, by basic visualization 26
exploring, by end-user interfaces 42
exploring by graphs, in Rattle 44
exploring, in Rattle 43
loading, into Rattle 42
relations, exploring in 39-44
rescaling 48, 49
transforming 48
data mining 2
data mining methodology 10
dataset
exploring 17-26
loading 14-16
dendextend
reference link 164
devtools
about 132
reference link 165
distance metric
about 71
Binary Distance 71
Canberra Distance 71
Correlation 72
Euclidean Distance 71
Manhattan Distance 71
Maximum Distance 71
Pearson Distance 72
Spearman Distance 72
divisive methods 70
dplyr
reference link 162

E

ElemStatLearn
reference link 163
embedded methods, subset selection techniques 152-154
end-user interfaces
data, exploring by 42

entropy 7
ewkm 153
expert knowledge-based techniques 149
exploratory data analysis 14

F

factoextra
about 132
reference link 132
Factominer
reference link 141
Factoshiny
reference link 165
fBasics
reference link 162
feature extraction 114
feature ranking 149-152
feature selection techniques
about 148
benefits 148
filter methods, subset selection techniques 157-159
fpc
reference link 164
FSelector
reference link 166

G

ggplot2
reference link 162
gplots
reference link 162

H

HCPC function 137
hierarchical clustering
about 70
distance metric, clustering 71, 72
in R 73-78
linkage methods 72
on principal components 137-139
plotting alternatives 84-88
tips, for selecting 81-83
with factors 79, 80

Hierarchical Clustering Analysis (HCA) 70
histogram
   about 27
   building 27-30
Hmisc
   reference link 162
HSAUR
   reference link 164

I

imputation missing data
   about 55
   mean imputation 57, 58
   Zero/Missing 56
information age 2
information gain 8, 9
information theory 6
Iris dataset 16

K

K-Means Clustering
   about 58-62
   clusters number, defining 62-67

L

labels 3
lattice
   reference link 163
linkage methods
   about 72
   Average Linkage 72
   Centroid Linkage 72
   Complete Linkage 72
   McQuitty Linkage 72
   Median Linkage 72
   Single Linkage 72
   Ward Linkage 72

M

machine learning
   about 1-3
   supervised learning 3, 4
   unsupervised learning 5, 6

mclust
   reference link 166
mean imputation 57, 58
Median/MAD 54
Multiple Correspondence Analysis
   (MCA) 132

N

natural log 55
NbClust
   reference link 163
normalization techniques
   Median/MAD 54
   natural log 55
   recenter 49-52
   Scale [0-1] 52, 53

P

pastecs
   reference link 162
plotting alternatives, for association
   rules 106
Principal component analysis (PCA)
   about 111, 115
   advanced tools, for plotting 132-136
   by user interfaces 140-144
   visual support 128-131
principal components
   calculating 115-127
   calculating, correlation matrix used 115
   calculating, covariance matrix used 115
princomp 118

R

R
   benefits 11
   reference link 162
Rattle
   data, exploring by graphs 44
   data, exploring in 43
   data, loading into 42
   relations, exploring in data 44
   reference link 163
Rcmdr
   reference link 165

Rcpp
  reference link 165
recenter 49-52
relations
  exploring, in data 39-44
reshape
  reference link 163

S

Scale [0-1] 52, 53
scatterplot3d
  reference link 163
silhouette graphics
  reference link 70
singular value decomposition (SVD) 117
software tools, data mining
  CRISP-DM 10, 11
special visualizations 35-38
SphericalCubature 113
stringi
  reference link 165
subset selection techniques
  about 152
  embedded methods 152-154
  filter methods 157-159
  wrapper methods 154-156
supervised learning
  about 3
  modeling stage 4
  models 4
  predicting stage 5

U

UCI Machine Learning Repository
  reference link 73
unsupervised learning 5, 6

V

visual support, on PCA 128-131

W

within-cluster sum of squares (WCSS) 58
wrapper methods, subset selection
    techniques 154-156
wskm
  reference link 166

X

XLConnect
  reference link 162

Thank you for buying
Unsupervised Learning with R

About Packt Publishing

Packt, pronounced 'packed', published its first book, *Mastering phpMyAdmin for Effective MySQL Management*, in April 2004, and subsequently continued to specialize in publishing highly focused books on specific technologies and solutions.

Our books and publications share the experiences of your fellow IT professionals in adapting and customizing today's systems, applications, and frameworks. Our solution-based books give you the knowledge and power to customize the software and technologies you're using to get the job done. Packt books are more specific and less general than the IT books you have seen in the past. Our unique business model allows us to bring you more focused information, giving you more of what you need to know, and less of what you don't.

Packt is a modern yet unique publishing company that focuses on producing quality, cutting-edge books for communities of developers, administrators, and newbies alike. For more information, please visit our website at www.packtpub.com.

About Packt Open Source

In 2010, Packt launched two new brands, Packt Open Source and Packt Enterprise, in order to continue its focus on specialization. This book is part of the Packt Open Source brand, home to books published on software built around open source licenses, and offering information to anybody from advanced developers to budding web designers. The Open Source brand also runs Packt's Open Source Royalty Scheme, by which Packt gives a royalty to each open source project about whose software a book is sold.

Writing for Packt

We welcome all inquiries from people who are interested in authoring. Book proposals should be sent to author@packtpub.com. If your book idea is still at an early stage and you would like to discuss it first before writing a formal book proposal, then please contact us; one of our commissioning editors will get in touch with you.

We're not just looking for published authors; if you have strong technical skills but no writing experience, our experienced editors can help you develop a writing career, or simply get some additional reward for your expertise.

Learning Predictive Analytics with R

ISBN: 978-1-78216-935-2   Paperback: 332 pages

Get to grips with key data visualization and predictive analytic skills using R

1. Acquire predictive analytic skills using various tools of R.

2. Make predictions about future events by discovering valuable information from data using R.

3. Comprehensible guidelines that focus on predictive model design with real-world data.

Python Machine Learning

ISBN: 978-1-78355-513-0   Paperback: 454 pages

Unlock deeper insights into machine learning with this vital guide to cutting-edge predictive analytics

1. Leverage Python's most powerful open-source libraries for deep learning, data wrangling, and data visualization.

2. Learn effective strategies and best practices to improve and optimize machine learning systems and algorithms.

3. Ask – and answer – tough questions of your data with robust statistical models, built for a range of datasets.

Please check **www.PacktPub.com** for information on our titles

Mastering Machine Learning with R

ISBN: 978-1-78398-452-7   Paperback: 400 pages

Master machine learning techniques with R to deliver complex and robust projects

1. Get to grips with the application of Machine Learning methods using an extensive set of R packages.

2. Understand the benefits and potential pitfalls of using machine learning methods.

3. Implement the numerous powerful features offered by R with this comprehensive guide to building an independent R-based ML system.

Machine Learning with R
Second Edition

ISBN: 978-1-78439-390-8   Paperback: 452 pages

Discover how to build machine learning algorithms, prepare data, and dig deep into data prediction techniques with R

1. Harness the power of R for statistical computing and data science.

2. Explore, forecast, and classify data with R.

3. Use R to apply common machine learning algorithms to real-world scenarios.

Please check **www.PacktPub.com** for information on our titles

19994610R00107

Printed in Great Britain
by Amazon